The Crisis in American Banking

The Political Economy of the Austrian School

General Editor: Mario J. Rizzo
New York University

Although long associated with a deep appreciation of the free market, the Austrian School has not been recognized fully as a unique approach in analyzing the role of government in the economy. A major contribution of the Austrian School was to demonstrate, as early as 1920, the impossibility of economic calculation under socialism. Recent events in the former Soviet Union and Eastern Europe have dramatically illustrated the cogency of this argument. In more recent times and in contrast to conventional static analyses, Austrian research has been concerned with the impact of government control on entrepreneurial discovery. To what extent does the impact of such control go beyond the firm's static pricing decision and reach into the very discovery of new opportunities and hence the transmission of knowledge in society? Austrians are also concerned with the dynamics of state intervention—the degree to which one intervention induces further interventions and, conversely, the degree to which one decontrol "necessitates" further steps in the process of deregulation. Finally, the Austrian School is firmly committed to the value-freedom of economics, that is, the separation of the analysis of policy consequences from the moral and political values inherent in the *advocacy* of particular economic policies.

The Crisis in American Banking

Edited by
Lawrence H. White

New York University Press
New York and London

NEW YORK UNIVERSITY PRESS
New York and London

This book has been sponsored in part by
the Austrian Economics Program at New York University.

Library of Congress Cataloging-in-Publication Data
The Crisis in American banking / edited by Lawrence H. White.
p. cm.—(The Political economy of the Austrian school)
Includes bibliographical reference and index.
ISBN 0-8147-9260-X
1. Banks and banking—United States. 2. Banks and banking—United States—State supervision. 3. Banks and banking—United States—Deregulation. 4. Deposit insurance—United States. I. White, Lawrence H. II. Series.
HG2491.C75 1993
332.1'0973—dc20 92-45762
CIP

New York University Press books are printed on acid-free paper,
and their binding materials are chosen for strength and durability.

Manufactured in the United States of America

c 10 9 8 7 6 5 4 3 2 1

Contents

Foreword

Mario J. Rizzo

This book, *The Crisis in American Banking*, is the first in a new series of books that will be published under the rubric of the "Political Economy of the Austrian School." The essays collected here are the revised versions of papers presented at a conference at New York University on April 29, 1991. The financial support for this conference was provided by the Sarah Scaife Foundation. We are indebted to the foundation and its president, Richard M. Larry, for generous support, not only of this conference but also of the Austrian Economics Program at New York University over a period of many years. Further debts to Professor Lawrence H. White of the Department of Economics, University of Georgia, for his assistance in organizing the conference and editing the proceedings, and to New York University for providing convenient conference facilities, are gratefully acknowledged.

The Crisis in American Banking

Introduction

Lawrence H. White

This volume offers six original essays keyed to the continuing crisis in the U.S. banking industry. Five were first presented at a small conference—more like a series of seminars—on "The Crisis in the Banking Industry," sponsored by NYU's Austrian Economics Program (which is directed by Israel Kirzner). The conference was organized by Mario Rizzo and myself, and was held at New York University on April 29, 1991. The papers generated lively discussion among the authors and other participants in the conference, and have been revised to reflect (or deflect) constructive criticism received there. A sixth paper, by Richard Salsman, was solicited soon after the conference. All six have been updated to reflect developments through September 1991.

The U.S. banking system, its regulation and deregulation, and its troubles, have been much in the news lately. Banking topics have been discussed by economists in a number of monographs and conference volumes. The rationale for adding the present volume to the discussion is the hope that its contributors provide fresh perspectives by viewing the banking scene from unusual angles. In particular, several authors draw ideas from modern Austrian economics or from public choice theory that have seldom been applied to explaining contemporary banking problems.

A pervasive theme of the contributions here is that the U.S. banking crisis is fundamentally linked to the political regulation of banking. (Popular alternative explanations point to supposedly excessive competition or deregulation in banking, or to a supposed decline in the ethical standards of bankers in the 1980s.) Taken together, the chapters below (1) indicate that government regulatory, macroeconomic, and fiscal policies have seriously impaired the health of the banking industry; (2) contribute to explaining how rent-seeking, ideology, and the historical accretion of regulations have given banking policy its current unfortunate form; and (3) consider the long-term prospects for reform of banking regulation, and for the banking industry itself in light of the current and foreseeable regulatory environment.

In the first chapter I attempt to provide an overview of the U.S. banking industry's troubles and the FDIC's insolvency, and to trace them to regulatory and macroeconomic policies. The secularly shrinking profits brought to banking by techological change, as discussed in this volume by George Kaufman, explain why the banking industry should contract, but not why its contraction should be punctuated by a crisis involving high levels of loan losses and bank failures. I suggest that cyclical losses in bank lending, especially severe today in the area of real estate lending, represent correlated errors induced by unpredictable monetary policy. Regulation (particulary restrictions on geographic and product-line diversification) and deposit insurance explain why U.S. banks, as the thrifts did earlier, have reacted to a downturn with increased risk taking. Increased risk taking has led to dramatic exits in the fashion of the Bank of New England, rather than simple shrinkage or redeployment of capital. Policy reform should seek to remove the distortions that promote excessive risk taking.

Roger Garrison addresses the impact of government budget deficits on the economy in general and on banking in particular. He argues that unusually large borrowing, to cover today's deficit, forces market participants to guess about tomorrow's policy for servicing or repaying the debt, and to guess about how other market participants will view the situation and respond. To what extent will a continued debt burden absorb domestic saving, causing high real interest rates and crowding out domestic investment? To what extent will it absorb funds from abroad, keeping real interest rates at their normal level but weakening demand for export goods? To what extent will taxes be raised, when, and on what? To what extent will the debt be monetized, causing inflation? Deriving surprising illumination from standard national-income accounting, Garrison shows that some combination of these (jointly exhaustive) repercussions must follow a deficit.

Empirical studies may show no strong or regular connection between deficits and any *one* of these repercussions, but Garrison points out that it would be fallacious to conclude that deficits have no repercussions or are harmless. The lack of a predictable mix of repercussions in fact means that market participants face added uncertainty. This excess uncertainty hinders decision making in the banking sector—portfolios will prove to have been misallocated when guesses about answers to the above questions prove to have been mistaken, or rates of return will be reduced by greater hedging—and in the rest of the economy.

Thomas Havrilesky examines the role of private interests (the S&L and big-bank lobbies) in shaping banking legislation between 1985 and 1987, a period in which thrift industry problems incubated. In provocative language he argues that banking- and thrift-industry policy, like politics generally, is about "rent-seeking" or redistributing income. Critical changes in the regulatory rules governing S&Ls in the 1980s (an increase in the deposit insurance ceiling, regulatory forbearance to close insolvent thrifts, relaxed accounting standards) appear to reflect the capture of legislators and regulators by the S&L lobby. Studying the statistical relationship between a Congressperson's contributions from S&L or big-bank lobbies (Political Action Committees, or PACs) and his or her voting or bill sponsorship, Havrilesky finds evidence that each lobby was influential. Congresspeople who sponsored pro-big-bank bills received a bigger share of their PAC money from big-bank PACs; those who voted as the S&L lobby preferred likewise received greater proportionate S&L PAC contributions.

Popular accounts of the thrift-industry fiasco, and of the FDIC's current difficulties, have blamed fraud and mismanagement among bankers, citing anecdotal evidence of renegades like Charles Keating. Richard Salsman's essay provides a useful historical perspective by showing that the same sort of charges were made in previous U.S. banking crises: the "wildcat banking" episodes of the antebellum period; the money panics of the National Banking era, especially the Panic of 1907; the banking collapse of the Great Depression; and the S&L crisis of the 1980s. In each case bankers were blamed for ills that Salsman—drawing on important "revisionist" work by monetary theorists and historians in the last twenty years—indicates should in fact be traced to government interference in banking. Legal restrictions, in the later episodes combined with central banking and deposit insurance, have created climates in which unsafe banking practices can persist and become institutionalized. He concludes that systemic bad banking is a symptom of bad policy, rather than an independent cause of crisis.

Why then have bankers been made scapegoats? Salsman cites a number of cases in which federal legislators, agency heads, and commissioners have led the movement to blame bankers, rather than government policies, for the banking system's failings. Self-interest provides an obvious motive. A question that remains to be answered is why the popular press have not been more discerning.

Walker Todd and Gerald P. O'Driscoll, Jr., provide further evidence of the destabilizing effects of government deposit guarantees. They emphasize that explicit deposit insurance is only one part of the "safety net" whose historical growth they document; implicit guarantees are an additional and crucial part. They warn that government supervisory agencies will not rein in excessive risk taking by banks (being inherently prone to err on the side of wishful thinking) until it is too late. Political pressures will then be brought to bear on the supervisors (the FDIC and the Fed) to bail out failing institutions, as long as deposit guarantees of any amount are in effect. They find evidence of these pressures not only in the much-discussed doctrine that some banks are "too big to fail" but also in the abuse of the Fed's discount window for bank rescues, a feature of the current system that has scarcely been mentioned elsewhere. The central bank discount window, under classical lender of last resort doctrine, is supposed to provide only liquidity support to the banking system, not capital support to individual insolvent institutions. Walker and O'Driscoll note that Fed loans to banks declared insolvent are repaid out of the FDIC's Bank Insurance Fund, and the BIF is ultimately replenished with taxpayer money, so the current system "converts unsound banking policy use of the discount window to keep insolvent banks afloat into unsound fiscal policy." They conclude that to achieve stability the entire safety net needs to be reformed, not only deposit insurance.

Todd and O'Driscoll argue for a comprehensive set of reforms that would eliminate federal deposit guarantees. At the very least, they favor a bank closure policy that exposes depositors and shareholders, but not taxpayers, to losses. Observing that the deposit guarantee system will soon be transferring wealth from the average citizen (through taxation to recapitalize the FDIC) to the wealthy citizen (who has parked savings in insured deposits), they reasonably suggest that having an FDIC makes the average citizen worse off.

Risk-free savings vehicles paying competitive rates are already available in the form of Treasury bills and savings bonds.

Looking beyond the current crisis, George Kaufman surveys the secular trends that are shrinking the banking industry in comparison to other financial service providers. He finds that these trends stem partly from technological changes (such as advances in telecommunications and computerization), and partly from bad policy decisions (such as mispriced deposit insurance, forbearance to close insolvent institutions, and geographic and product-line restrictions). Shrinkage of the banking industry due to loss of comparative advantage is efficient and nothing to mourn. But shrinkage due to ill-conceived public policy is not efficient. Kaufman calls for correctly pricing deposit insurance, and for removing restrictions on the geographic and product-line powers of banks. He warns against softening the balance-sheet standards for banks, which some voices have urged as a way to combat a supposed "credit crunch." With broader powers but without subsidies, efficient U.S. banks should be able to compete on a level playing field. The success of foreign banks and nondepository financial firms in recent years shows that lesser deposit guarantees (and correspondingly higher capital ratios) do not preclude growth.

As this preface is written, the state of the U.S. commercial banking industry and the FDIC continues to suggest disturbing parallels to the state of the savings and loan industry and the FSLIC a decade earlier. With the BIF's balances down to $2 billion in late 1991 (less than the amount needed to close the Bank of New England earlier in the year), the FDIC appeared to be putting off closing banks that were insolvent (on a market-value accounting basis, i.e., when counting their assets at market value rather than book value). After predicting earlier in the year that 180 to 230 institutions would be seized in 1991, the FDIC reduced its estimate in December to only 137. In pleading for "recapitalization" of the BIF, FDIC chairman William Taylor acknowledged in so many words that lack of funds was hindering the agency from closing unsound banks. Such a policy of forbearance carries the danger of duplicating in banking the second phase of the thrift crisis, that is, of creating a new cohort of "zombie" institutions rationally pursuing risky strategies at the expense of future taxpayers who pick up the tab for losses by government deposit insurance agencies.

In November 1991 the FDIC's Bank Insurance Fund was "recapitalized" by omnibus banking legislation granting the agency an additional $70 billion in borrowing authority. The FDIC Improvement Act requires the FDIC to repay any borrowings from its asset sales or insurance premiums. It remains to be seen whether the agency will be able to repay, or whether taxpayers will be presented with the tab at a later date. The legislation includes a number of deposit insurance reforms: changes in accounting and examination rules; a schedule of restrictions to be placed on undercapitalized instutitions; a mandate for the FDIC to impose risk-based insurance premiums by 1994; and a requirement that the agency resolve failures by the method generating the least cost to the FDIC, even if that means exposing uninsured depositors to losses, beginning 1995. Proposals for structural reform of banking, to eliminate geographic and product-line restrictions, were excluded from the legislation.

With its new access to funds, the FDIC is expected to begin working off a backlog of insolvent but not-yet-seized institutions. The agency officially expects to close 200 to 239 banks, with total book assets in the neighborhood of $100 billion, in 1992 alone. Private analysts estimate $50 billion in losses to the FDIC from the closure of some 150 sick savings banks in New York and New England, in addition to losses from closure of ailing commercial banks. As the situation unfolds, observers who currently fear a replay of the $150 billion FSLIC bailout may find that they were overly pessimistic—or overly optimistic. Either way, the policy regime that allowed both the earlier and later problems to develop does not seem to be on the verge of any dramatic change. The reluctance of Congress to enact real reforms means that the critical analyses and reform proposals in this volume, against the wishes of their authors, will remain relevant for some time to come.

1

Why Is the U.S. Banking Industry in Trouble? Business Cycles, Loan Losses, and Deposit Insurance

Lawrence H. White

We learned from the U.S. thrift-industry debacle that congresspeople and regulators have incentives to mask and deny the size of insolvencies among deposit-taking institutions when they first arise. Rather than promptly resolve the widespread insolvencies that existed among thrifts in 1981, the authorities chose to revise the regulatory accounting rules, to practice "forbearance," and to gamble that economically insolvent thrifts might climb back into the black (Eisenbeis 1990, 19–20). As it turned out, the cost of resolving the problem grew, to the point where taxpayers have been saddled with an enormous expense in covering the thrift deposit guarantees made by the late FSLIC. Estimates of the expense, beginning at $10 billion in 1986, have been revised upward steadily to more than $150 billion (as of 1991, excluding interest).

The Industry's and the FDIC's Troubles Are Large

In light of this experience, a sense of déjà vu accompanied news reports, beginning in late 1990, that the Federal Deposit Insurance Corporation, the agency that now guarantees both thrift and bank deposits, would soon run out of money without taxpayer assistance. The FDIC's Bank Insurance Fund shrank as its annual disbursements in resolving bank failures, whose numbers swelled tremen-

Figure 1.1
Annual U.S. Bank Failures
1960–1990

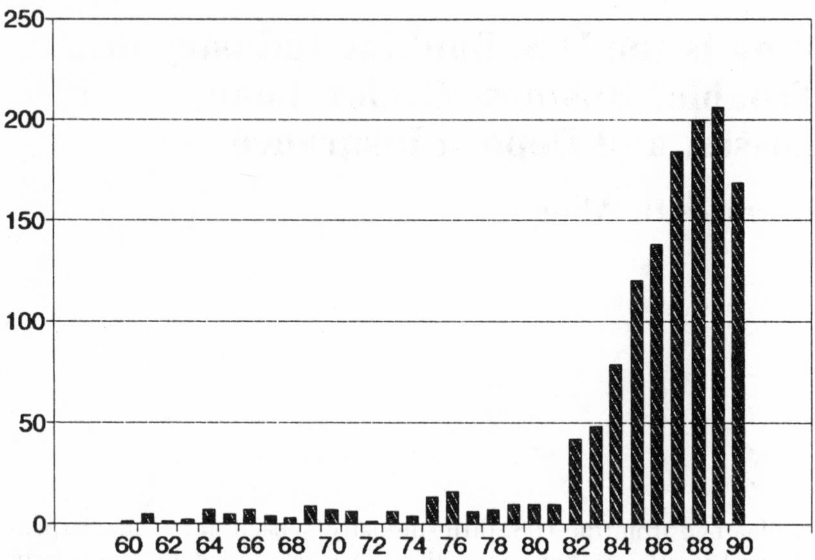

dously the last decade (see figure 1.1), exceeded its income from deposit insurance premiums. Beginning 1988 with $18.3 billion, the BIF lost $5.1 billion in 1988–89, and another $6.8 billion in 1990 alone, leaving its balance at only $6.4 billion at year-end 1990. The most recent FDIC projections imply net losses for 1991–92 of $19 to $38 billion.[1]

As they did with the FSLIC, the authorities have persistently underestimated the FDIC's problems. Early in 1990 FDIC officials projected that the agency would break even for the year. By midyear they projected 1990 losses of $2 billion. In September 1990 FDIC chairman William Seidman raised the estimate to $3 billion. In retrospect the FDIC first found that it had actually lost $4.8 billion in 1990 (the BIF's balances had declined to $8.4 billion at year-end 1990 from $13.2 billion at year-end 1989); later it revised the year-end 1990 balance to $6.4 billion, implying 1990 losses of $6.8 billion.[2]

The federal Office of Management and Budget projected in September 1990 that the FDIC would need infusions of $22.5 billion over the next five years to remain afloat. In October 1990, Seidman professed not to see the FDIC fund in danger for the foreseeable future, maintaining that the fund would remain in the black through the end of 1991. As 1991 began Seidman was asking Congress for a $10 billion loan to provide a margin of safety, though he had previously indicated that the fund could use a $25 billion infusion. The Congressional Budget Office projected in January 1991 that the BIF would develop a $2.8 billion deficit by mid-1992, but that (with increases in premiums) it would return to solvency by mid-1994. In March 1991 the Bush administration proposed that Congress provide the FDIC with $25 billion in borrowing authority. Within a week Seidman testified that under a "pessimistic economic scenario" the fund might have to borrow $30 to $35 billion, and the administration's request for FDIC borrowing authority was increased to $70 billion, just in case.[3] As of June 1991, the FDIC's "baseline projection" gave the BIF a year-end 1991 balance of $3.2 billion, while its "pessimistic scenario" projected a year-end balance of $1.7 billion. By the fall of 1991 it was evident that even the "pessimistic scenario" was overly optimistic. Seidman was projecting that the fund would be insolvent at year's end, and reported that it had already borrowed $2.9 billion from the U.S. Treasury.[4]

As in the thrift meltdown, the projections of private-sector experts have been more pessimistic *ex ante* and have proven to be more accurate *ex post*. Bank consultant David Cates projected in October 1990, before the recession had been officially declared underway, that in a recession banks could lose $86.3 billion in equity, 41% of the industry's cushion, and taxpayers could face a bill as high as $40 billion to cover FDIC losses. Cates's credibility was enhanced by his projecting that, under such a scenario, the Bank of New England would fail. The Bank of New England failed in January 1991, amidst depositor runs, with losses expected to make it (at $2.5 billion) the third most expensive resolution in the FDIC's history. Lowell Bryan, a bankwatcher at McKinsey and Company, similarly projected in December 1990 that the FDIC would need injections of $20–40 billion over the next few years. A study by the independent bank rating service Veribanc found that the FDIC was already insolvent at year-end 1990, facing resolution costs for then-insolvent banks (estimated at $11.6 billion) in excess of BIF balances. Edward Kane estimated in mid-1991 that the BIF was already $40 billion in the hole as of the end of 1990, if one recognized as a BIF liability the negative net worth that would appear under mark-to-market accounting for insured banks' assets.[5]

An authoritative study of the FDIC's condition appeared in a report by James R. Barth, R. Dan Brumbaugh, and Robert E. Litan, dated December 1990, commissioned by the Financial Institutions Subcommittee of the House Banking Committee. Barth, Brumbaugh, and Litan (1990, 6) concluded that the BIF at the end of 1990 appeared to be where the FSLIC was in the mid-1980s, "without sufficient resources to pay for its expected caseload of failed depositories." The authors rehearsed a number of scenarios, varying in the assumed severity of the incipient recession and the degree of forbearance to be exercised toward larger banks.

They estimated (Barth, Brumbaugh, and Litan, 93, 103) that even under a "mild recession" the FDIC's bank resolution costs for 1991–93 would run between $31 and $43 billion, exhausting its expected resources of $28–31 billion (consisting of start-of-period reserves of $9 billion plus premium and interest income of $19–22 billion).

A major source of concern is that larger banks have begun to appear on the FDIC's list of "problem banks." The list numbered 975 banks at the midpoint of 1991, slightly fewer than in the immediately preceding years, but the aggregate assets of problem banks had increased. Likewise, although the number of bank failures in the first half of 1991 (fifty-seven) was fewer than in the first half of the previous year (ninety-nine), the average asset size of failed banks was much much larger: $475 million versus only $65 million (FDIC 1991, 2, 4).

In fact some of the very largest U.S. banks are teetering. *The Economist* commented in December 1990: "Nobody knows just how much rubbish [U.S.] banks have on their books, or how many loans might become rubbish if a recession deepens. Among the banks that fail may be prominent money-centres."[6] Barth, Brumbaugh, and Litan (1990, 13) commented that as of the end of 1990 "most" of the nation's largest banks were "on—or conceivably over—the edge of insolvency. . . . [M]any of these banks not only currently have weak balance sheets by any reasonable standard, but they also are highly exposed to additional deterioration in their capital positions from their significant involvement in high-risk lending."[7] They reported (Barth, Brumbaugh, and Litan 1990, 50) that six of the top twenty-five bank holding companies had "high risk loans" (loans for highly leveraged transactions [HLT], medium and long-term LDC loans, and commercial real estate loans) in excess of four times their "adjusted tangible common equity" (tangible common equity plus allowance for loan losses less 1% of all performing loans). That is, a

25% fall in the value of such a bank's high-risk loan portfolio, together with a normal 1% loss rate on other loans, would wipe out its capital, leaving it insolvent.

FDIC call reports show that the large banks (those with more than $10 billion in assets) as a size class have the weakest loan portfolios. Across most categories of loans, the large banks have the highest percentages of loans past due or noncurrent, and the highest percentage of loan charge-offs (FDIC 1991, 3). In recent years the class of large banks has had the highest percentage losing money. In the first half of 1991, 11.2% of all banks (1,361 of 12,150) lost money, while 19.6% of large banks (9 of 46) did so (FDIC 1991, 5).

Marketplace reflections of troubles at the large money-center banks are not hard to find. In 1980 Moody's Investors Services rated the debt of fourteen major banks "AAA"; today it gives only one U.S. bank that rating (Salsman 1990, 71). Moody's now rates a fifth of Chase Manhattan's debt even below investment grade (Byron 1990, 16). Stock traders' expectations of likely future difficulties in banking are reflected in low share prices (relative to current reported earnings) for all banks, but especially for large banks (Barth, Brumbaugh, and Litan 1990, 15). While healthier banks trade at slightly above book value, money center banks have been trading well below (Salsman 1990, 72).

In addition to the asset-quality problems at large banks, Barth, Brumbaugh, and Litan (1990, 51) pointed out that the Bank Insurance Fund is also threatened by renewed troubles at savings banks. They noted that BIF-insured savings banks in the aggregate lost $670 million in 1989. The latest available figures show the situation worsening. The number of "problem" savings banks, which stood at thirty-one in mid-1990, had risen to fifty-eight a year later. Savings banks in the aggregate dropped a staggering $2.5 billion in 1990, and lost another $662 million in the first half of 1991, exceeding losses in the first half of 1990. In New England, where most savings banks are located, two-thirds of the twenty-three largest institutions were unprofitable in the first half of 1991 (FDIC 1991, 7).

With the FDIC running out of cash, there is a great danger that the agency is neglecting to close insolvent banks, just as the FSLIC neglected insolvent thrifts for years. "Zombie" institutions (economically "dead" but still operating) may be afoot, piling up obligations that will eventually be laid at the doorstep of taxpayers. Barth, Brumbaugh, and Litan (1990, 81) note that during the years 1980–85, with fewer annual failures, the typical failed bank was resolved about fifteen months after it first appeared on the FDIC's problem list. By 1987–89, amidst two hundred failures per year, the typical failed bank was not resolved for 21–28 months after first being listed.

The Immediate Source of Trouble Is Bad Loans

U.S. banks are failing or troubled primarily because so many of the risky loans they made in the 1980s are in default. In the four quarters ending September 30, 1990, the banks' net charge-offs for bad loans were $30.5 billion, the largest dollar amount for any four-quarter period ever, and a record high percentage of assets. Charge-offs in the first half of 1991 continued at roughly the same high rate. Despite the charge-offs, the proportion of troubled loans on bank portfolios continued to rise. At the end of September 1990, the total of noncurrent loans and leases plus "other real estate owned" (foreclosed mortgage property) was $89.6 billion, up by $14.2 billion (19%) from a year earlier ($75.4 billion), and at a record level as a share (2.65%) of total assets (*FDIC* 1990, 1–3). By the midpoint of 1991, the total ($107.9) and the share (3.19%) had both risen even higher.

Despite the taking of historically large loan-loss provisions in 1989 and 1990, another round of large provisions was needed in 1991, and still another round was expected to be needed in 1992. Loan-loss reserves were down to 65 cents per dollar of noncurrent loans as of 1991:2, down from 73 cents as of 1990:3, and down from 83 cents a year before that. Losses from commercial real estate loans, LDC loans, and HLT loans were expected to increase in the recession, especially among the larger northeastern banks (*FDIC* 1990, 2).

The nature of the banking industry's bad loans has been widely reported. Southwestern banks, making up the majority of failed banks in the last few years, suffered big real-estate and energy loan losses in the late 1980s. The big money-center banks took sizable write-downs of LDC loans in 1987, such that all large banks posted negative returns for the year, and another milder round of write-downs in 1989. In both years, loss provisions on overseas loans more than accounted for the total negative income recorded; domestic business was profitable (Duca and McLaughlin 1990, 483). In 1989 through 1991, New England banks took large losses on real estate loans. Depressed real estate markets are pushing the value of much of the collateral held by banks below the value of the loans carried on many banks' books (Barth, Brumbaugh, and Litan 1990, 47), so that more loan defaults are expected. Bank inventories of foreclosed real estate were still accumulating as of mid-1991 (FDIC 1991, 2).

The Causes of Loan Losses Are Cyclical, Secular, and Regulatory

How can we explain the profile shown by figure 1.1, an extraordinary growth in the annual number of bank failures after 1981? Commercial bank profitability has trended downward since 1970 (FRBNY 1986), a trend that has continued in recent years and is consistent with banking firms exiting from the market. But the gradual secular trend in bank profitability cannot plausibly explain the dramatic shift in the trend of bank failures, or why it occurred when it did. The onset of a sharp recession in the second half of 1981 undoubtedly helped swell the number of failures in 1982 and 1983. But we clearly cannot explain the pattern solely by reference to the business cycle. The number of failures was much less in previous recessions, and failures continued to climb even after the 1982–83 recession gave way to a period of sustained expansion.

Cyclical Factors

A recession swells the number of bank failures for obvious asset-quality reasons. With unemployment up, more household loans go bad. As recession took hold in 1990, delinquency rates in home-improvement loans and revolving credit reached their highest levels in ten years (Farrell 1991, 29). More importantly, with corporate bankruptcies, business loans go bad. In the 1982–83 recession, energy and agricultural business loans especially went into default. In the most recent downswing, commercial property loans have been the most conspicuous source of losses and were the principal reason that the Bank of New England failed.

It would be myopic, however, to treat the recessionary phase of the cycle as the ultimate source or the exogenous cause of asset-quality problems. The loans that go bad were typically made years earlier during the expansion. Hundreds of banks had asset-quality problems well before the 1990–91 recession officially began, and bad assets brought on the 1988–89 wave of Texas bank failures in advance of the national recession. Viewing the upsurge in loan losses *ex post*, we see a "cluster of error" in bank lending: overexpansion in certain loan categories (LDC loans, commercial real estate, HLT loans), or overoptimism regarding their repayment prospects.[8] At the end of 1990:3, real estate assets (real estate loans plus mortgage-backed securities plus foreclosed properties) comprised 30.6% of total commercial bank assets, up from only 18.8% at end of 1984 (FDIC 1990, 1–2). Overbuilding in commercial real estate was evident from office vacancy rates, which approached 20% in many cities (Mandel 1991, 30). Analysts at the Federal Reserve Board (Duca and McLaughlin 1990, 487) noted that "concerns about the quality of real estate loans appear strongest in areas in which land prices had risen sharply in previous years."

This pattern—that recession is the sharpest where the expansion had previously been most vigorous—is consistent with "monetary malinvestment" theories of the business cycle, a class of theories that includes the work of the Austrian school in the 1920s and 1930s and that of Robert E. Lucas, Jr., in the 1970s and 1980s. As Lucas (1981, 9) has commented, this work insists on "the necessity of viewing [recurrent business cycles] as mistakes." The theoretical problem is then "to rationalize these mistakes as intelligent responses to movements in nominal 'signals' of movements in the underlying 'real' variables we care about and want to react to." That is, a monetary malivestment theory traces the clustered business failures and unemployment of the recession phase to decisions (retrospectively inappropriate) made by labor and capital owners during the expansion phase, and appeals to monetary disturbances to explain why these decisions appeared sensible at the time they were made.

Rational-expectations work in monetary business cycle theory emphasizes that unanticipated monetary expansion generates unexpectedly high nominal demand for outputs. The Austrian theorists emphasized that new money, injected into the loanable funds market, reduces real interest rates in the short run. Both effects misleadingly signal businesses that their real profitability has increased, and so spur the unsustainable real expansion that constitutes the boom period. Real interest rates (measured by the annualized nominal interest rate on three-month T-bills minus the contemporaneous annual inflation rate) in the United States fell during the 1970s, and were actually negative from 1974 through 1980 (Kohn 1991, 729). Merely holding inventories appeared to be profitable. With disinflation after 1980, real interest rates rose sharply, and nominal demand no longer outran expectations.

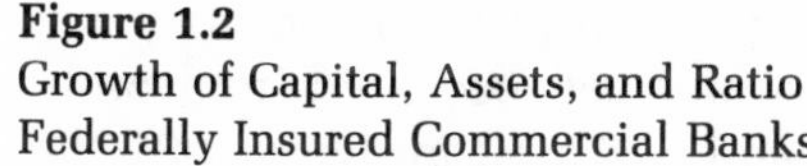

Figure 1.2
Growth of Capital, Assets, and Ratio
Federally Insured Commercial Banks

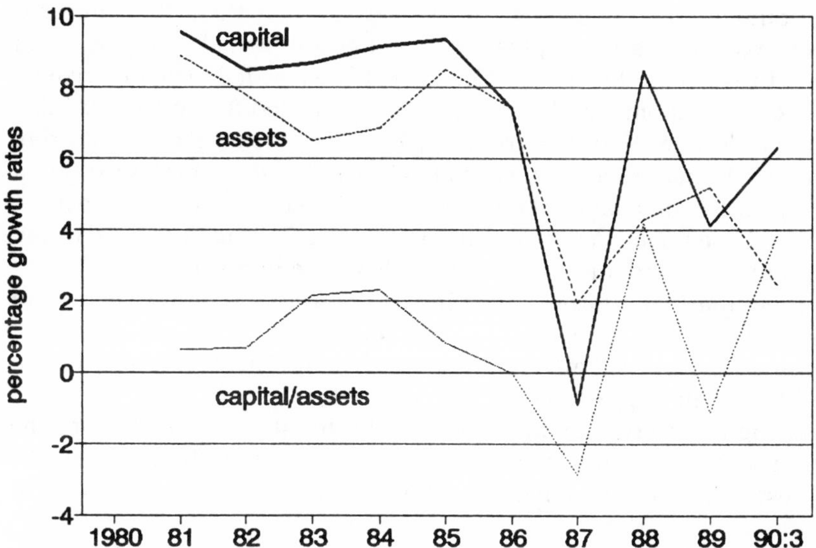

Richard Salsman (1990, 25–28) has offered the interesting hypothesis that U.S. banks may have been directly (as well as indirectly, via the business cycle) weakened by expansionary monetary policy. The Fed rapidly expanded the monetary base, leading in textbook fashion to the multiple expansion of bank deposits and loans. Meanwhile, Salsman argues, banks were not able to raise or internally generate enough capital to keep pace, so that their capital/asset ratios fell. This argument implies that movements in the banking industry's capital/asset ratio should be predominantly associated with movements in the denominator (assets), with the numerator (capital) remaining relatively stable. At least in the 1980s, however, industry aggregates do not show this pattern. Figure 1.2 plots year-to-year compound growth rates (differences in natural log levels) for capital, assets, and the capital-asset ratio. It shows that capital growth has been at least as volatile as asset growth.

Regional Factors

Various regions of the United States have taken turns being worst hit with bank asset-quality problems during recent quarters, but all except the Midwest and Central regions have been seriously hit. Southwestern banks' portfolios have not yet recovered from problems that came to a head in 1988 and 1989. At midyear 1991 the "troubled real estate asset rate" as measured by the FDIC ("noncurrent real restate loans plus other real estate owned as a percent of total real estate loans plus OREO") still exceeded 10% in Arizona, Texas, Oklahoma, and Louisiana and exceeded 8% in New Mexico and Colorado. Northeastern banks have had the biggest recent problems with real-estate loans. Troubled real estate asset rates exceeded 10% in Rhode Island, Massachusetts, Connecticut, New Hampshire, New Jersey, New York, and the District of Columbia and exceeded 8% in Maryland and Virginia. No other state in the nation had a rate exceeding 8%, and only four (Maine, Vermont, Pennsylvania, and Florida) had rates exceeding 6%. Nationally, 11.2% of banks lost money in the first half of 1991, but 25.7% in FDIC's Northeast region did so. The biggest increases in loan loss provisions were taken during that period by banks in the Northeast and in the West. The largest increase in noncurrent loans was recorded by banks in the West, where 19.2% of banks lost money.

Secularly Shrinking Profitability

For the aggregate of federally insured commercial banks, the ratio of net income to assets has declined from 0.68 for 1980–85 (the average of annual figures) to 0.53 for 1986–90:2 (Barth, Brumbaugh, and Litan 1990, 121).[9] At the lower tail of the earnings distribution, where net income can be negative, cumulative losses can deplete capital and cause insolvency. Some 354 banks have reported losses every year from 1986 to 1989 (Fromson 1990, 119).

Much has been written in recent years about the erosion of the profitability of commercial banking under the impact of competition from nonbank intermediaries and from securities markets. Securitization is estimated to have reduced the spread on residential mortgages by fifty to one hundred basis points (Barth, Brumbaugh, and Litan 1990, 116, citing Rosenthal and Ocampo 1988). Increasing numbers of corporations, especially those with better bond ratings than the money-center banks, find it cheaper to issue commercial paper to investors directly than to borrow from banks at traditional spreads. With deposit interest rate ceilings being lifted after 1980, there has also been greater price competition for deposits among banks and between banks and thrifts.

In light of this we should note the apparently contradictory view that observed spreads between deposit and loan interest rates have not shrunk. A Federal Reserve Bank of New York staff study of *Recent Trends in Commercial Bank Profitability* (1986, 16) declared that "despite all the structural changes relating to interest rates and interest rate competition of recent years, there has been no visible impact on the net interest margins of the banks." It is true that, abstracting from loan loss provisions, industry-wide net income has been stable as a share of assets (Duca and McLaughlin 1990, 477). Net interest income actually shows a slight upward trend over the 1980s, from 3.03% of assets in both 1980 and 1981, to 3.40% in both 1989 and the first half of 1990 (Barth, Brumbaugh, and Litan 1990, 121).

This only means, however, that in an accounting sense it is loan loss provisions, and not declining spreads as they are measured *ex ante*, that account for the decline in return on assets. Increasing loan loss provisions (typically a belated response to increasing default rates) reveal *ex post* that spreads actually have declined for loans of a given risk class. Loan loss rates have been rising more or less steadily since 1962 (Barth, Brumbaugh, and Litan 1990, 117, 119). Lower-quality loans have been booked at *ex ante* spreads that used to be reserved for higher-quality loans. Barth, Brumbaugh, and Litan (1990, 117) argue that the movement of blue-chip borrowers to the commercial paper market, making banks unable to place loans of the traditional sort, helps explain why banks have taken on the additional risk that is evident from rising loan losses. The loss of traditional borrowers does explain why commercial and industrial (C&I) loans fell from 21% of bank assets down to 19% over the course of the 1980s, to be replaced by loans with higher default risk. But it does not explain why banks, as Barth, Brumbaugh, and Litan (1990, 128) elsewhere document, chose to take on more *portfolio* risk over the course of the 1980s by reducing the share of cash and investment securities in their portfolios, or why they increased the share of real estate loans by more percentage points than the share of C&I loans declined. It does not explain why "within the real estate loan category, banks shifted toward the riskiest borrowers," namely construction and development loans and commercial mortgages.

Most importantly, the shrinkage of margins on traditional loans does not by itself explain why banks have *underpriced* loans to their new borrowers. That is, it does not explain why they collected *ex ante* spreads too small to preserve income net of loan losses except in those unlikely states of the world (which did not obtain) in which the new loan portfolios had no higher a default rate than the old. To explain this mistake we need either to explain why banks would have failed to perceive that default rates were likely to be higher, or we need to explain why they became more willing to take on portfolio risk.

The Roles of Regulation and Deposit Insurance

The roots of the thrift industry crisis in regulation and deposit insurance are now well understood (Kane 1985, 1989; Brumbaugh 1988; Benston and Kaufman 1986). A number of long-standing legal restrictions, particularly restrictions against product-line diversification, made (and still make) thrifts weaker and more vulnerable to adverse shocks than they would otherwise be. Such restrictions alone cannot explain why failures exploded in the 1980s, for they did not suddenly become more binding. But they help to explain why the adverse cyclical and secular factors discussed above brought down as many thrifts as they did.

In the most general terms, the surge of thrift failures in 1981–82 can be attributed to interest-rate risk.[10] By funding long-term fixed-rate mortgages with short-term deposits, thrifts were implicitly betting heavily against a large rise in interest rates. They lost the bet. The average explicit interest cost of savings deposits in FSLIC-insured institutions rose from 6.6% in 1978 to 11.2% in 1982 (Kane 1989, 12–13, table 1–2). Although interest rates on new mortgages also rose, the thrifts' assets consisted largely of conventional fixed-rate mortgage loans made in the 1960s and '70s, paying between 6% and 9%. Borrowing at 11% to fund old mortgages paying 6 to 9%, hundreds of thrifts soon found their equity consumed by negative income flows.

The thrift crisis continued (or a *second* thrift crisis arose), despite the fall in interest rates after 1982, because the regulators' failure to close literally hundreds of insolvent thrifts created an army of institutional "zombies," economically dead but not yet buried, that rationally gambled for "resurrection." In general terms, unclosed thrifts substituted credit risk for interest-rate risk. Long-odds gambling in the form of high-risk lending offered the owners of insolvent thrifts their best hope of getting back into the black, making their shares worth something again. The downside risk fell entirely on the FSLIC:

the owners of thrifts with zero net worth had literally nothing to lose. Cole, McKenzie, and White (1990) provide econometric evidence that thrift failures in the late 1980s were swelled by risk-taking strategies begun earlier in the decade, strategies motivated by low net worth and forbearance. Failed thrifts had riskier portfolios than nonfailed thrifts, namely, higher concentrations of nonresidential mortgages, land loans, and real estate investments. "Moral hazard" behavior is indicated by the lower failure probabilities for institutions whose ownership structures gave their managers less to gain from risk taking: mutual institutions compared to stock institutions, publicly traded stock institutions compared to closely held stock institutions. Failure probabilities were higher for banks with higher managerial expenses.

Competition from zombie thrifts, who bid deposit rates up and loan rates down, made survival more difficult for still-solvent thrifts. By 1986 the average explicit earnings spread on new mortgage loans was smaller than it had been since 1972, and the spread net of average thrift operating expenses had reached a historic low (Kane 1989, 12–13, table 1–2). The result was a mushrooming number of economically insolvent institutions (Kane 1989, 26, table 2–1) and an accumulation of red ink that finally exceeded the FSLIC's resources by hundreds of billions of dollars.

Because commercial banks were carrying less of a mismatch between the repricing frequencies of their assets and liabilities than were thrifts, the banks were less victimized by the run-up in the level of interest rates in 1979–82. But banks with large maturity mismatches (borrowing short to lend long) did suffer large losses because of frequently inverted yield curves (short rates above long rates) during the period (FRBNY 1986, 117–21). The yield curve returned to its normal slope in 1983. The number of problem banks grew steadily up to 1986, however, with the rising failure rate among commercial and industrial business and increasing loan losses. The secular trend toward declining spreads continued to exert itself.

The increasing number of banks approaching the brink of insolvency has meant, as it meant in the case of thrifts who reached or crossed the brink a few years earlier, an increased attraction to financial "gambling." Booking high-risk loans without premia sufficient to cover probable defaults is a way to maximize the expected value of the bank to its owners, given that the owners can pass losses in excess of equity on to the FDIC. Deposit insurance, in other words, has created in commercial banking the same two "moral hazard" problems that have been much discussed in connection with the second wave of the thrift industry crisis.

1. Insured depositors (de jure or de facto) do not discipline weak institutions by demanding higher deposit rates or by moving funds to stronger institutions. Riskier banks can essentially sell a lower-quality product at the same price because customers are fully covered against product failure. Without risk-sensitive insurance premiums as a substitute for depositor discipline, deposit insurance subsidizes risk taking. A bank's expected return on assets can be increased by taking on a riskier (higher-variance) loan portfolio, but its cost of funds does not rise even though the bank is more likely to fail. Maximizing expected net payoff therefore pushes the bank to a riskier position on the risk-return frontier than would be taken by a bank whose uninsured depositors demanded compensation for an increased risk of default on their claims, or by a bank whose insurer priced its premiums to reflect insolvency risk. Banks have accordingly chosen lower capital/asset ratios as deposit guarantees have grown in scope and in implicit value.

2. In combination with forbearance, deposit guarantees enable and encourage insolvent banks to gamble for resurrection from economic insolvency. An insolvent institution can bid for funds with little risk premium to try to grow back into the black. Its owners have everything to gain and, with FDIC absorbing the downside risk, nothing to lose. With enough forbearance they can even operate a Ponzi scheme, using new deposits to pay the interest on old deposits (Kaufman 1988, 574).

The U.S. system of deposit guarantees thus serves as a background condition explaining banks' risk-preference behavior: it encourages banks close to insolvency to take on greater risks. This "moral hazard" problem likely intensified in the 1980s because the effective coverage of deposit guarantees was extended, and because the guarantees were increasingly mispriced. The Depository Institutions Deregulation and Monetary Control Act of 1980 raised explicit deposit coverage to $100,000 per account, from $40,000. This made it cheaper for depositors to get full coverage for large amounts by spreading funds among banks, with or without the help of a broker, and correspondingly made it easier for risk-prone banks to acquire funds (Kaufman 1988, 574).

Perhaps more importantly, the FDIC extended *de facto* full coverage to all liability holders of large banks. The FDIC increasingly resolved bank failures by "purchase and assumption," arranging takeovers that fully protected uninsured liability holders from loss, as in the Franklin National Bank case in 1974. There still remained the threat that uninsured depositors might take losses if a bank had to be liquidated because it was in such bad shape that no purchaser could be found. The FDIC removed even that threat in the 1984 Continental Illinois case, when the FDIC itself effectively purchased (nationalized) the insolvent bank (O'Driscoll 1988, 666). The FDIC enunciated the so-called too big to fail doctrine, under which even uninsured liability holders would be protected from any loss. Consistent with the extension of de facto guarantees, Short and Robinson (1990, 14–15) note that while high-risk banks normally had to pay a premium rate to attract large uninsured CDs in the mid-1970s, studies of more recent data do not consistently show risk premia on CDs or subordinated debt. Finally, because banks' exposure to interest-rate risk increased with the increased volatility of interest rates in the 1980s, but their deposit insurance premiums did not, the risk subsidy implicit in FDIC guarantees increased (Benston and Kaufman 1986, 62).

Evidence of increased bank gambling can be found in the changing composition of bank portfolios. Cash and investment securities declined to only 27% of assets in 1990 from 36% in 1980. Loans rose to 61% of assets from 54%, real estate loans to 23% from 15%. Within real estate, as noted above, banks shifted toward riskier borrowers, namely construction and development loans and commercial mortgages (Barth, Brumbaugh, and Litan 1990, 128). In 1989, bank real estate loans exceeded C&I loans for the first time ever (Fromson 1990, 120). Further evidence of increased bank gambling can be seen in the rising cost of resolving failed institutions: 20.3% of deposits in 1989 failures, double the 10.2% figure for 1985 failures (Barth, Brumbaugh, and Litan 1990, 29, table 4). Higher resolution costs mean either that authorities were slower to close banks after their economic net worth crossed into the negative region, or that the banks' net worth fell more rapidly. Increased reliance on high-risk "double-or-nothing" lending strategies can have both effects. It can increase the discrepancy between the economic value of assets and their value according to regulatory accounting principles, so that authorities are slower to recognize negative net worth. And it can make asset values fall more rapidly because returns on high-risk assets are more sensitive to changes in the state of the world.

Just as competition from zombie thrifts impaired the profitability of solvent thrifts, competition from zombie banks has weakened solvent banks. These spillover effects are ironic, because the ostensible purpose of deposit insurance was to prevent spillover effects (namely the spread of runs) from unsound to sound banks. Short and Robinson (1990, 7–8) find that insolvent (but still open) Texas banks bid up the deposit rates paid by other Texas banks, and may have increased the number and size of insolvencies. They also point out that the FDIC policy of resolving institutions with assistance, absorbing bad assets to keep them open, puts unassisted institutions (who have to swallow their own bad assets) at a competitive disadvantage. Conversely, others have noted that the shrinkage of the thrift industry, in part due to RTC closures, has helped strengthen commercial banks by giving them retail deposits that are on average a cheaper source of funds than brokered deposits (Duca and McLaughlin 1990, 488).

Policy Implications

A banker quoted anonymously in the New York Fed study *Recent Trends in Commercial Bank Profitability* (FRBNY 1986, 43) explained clearly the incentive of an unprofitable bank to gamble for recovery:

> One banker said that traditional corporate banking faced two alternatives, both of which are "routes to going out of business." One is just to say "no" to underpriced risky deals. The other is to take the risks, the alternative most organizations are driven to by the need to occupy an existing staff of loans officers and supporting personnel. This latter alternative, he said, simply results in going out of business "more dramatically," especially in a disinflationary period when the inflation that temporarily hid the risks is no longer there to mask them.

Our current deposit guarantee system allows a bank to take the risks without a correspondingly greater cost of funds, despite the increased likelihood that it will exit the business "dramatically." We have seen all too many dramatic exits in recent years. Taxpayers have discovered that they are the financial "angels" obliged to cover the costs of what threatens to be a very expensive show.

A minimal goal for banking policy would be to give bankers the proper incentive to choose the less dramatic route to going out of business. A bank should be led to retire gracefully as its profitability declines, rather than to run up a bill for other banks, or taxpayers, in the course of fighting the inevitable. If market forces dictate that the banking industry as a whole is to shrink, let it not consume others' wealth in the process. Let it shrink quietly and promptly, so that financial resources can be reallocated with minimum waste to what promise to be more valuable uses.

The absence of incentives to gamble for resurrection can be seen in historical banking systems with unlimited liability for bank shareholders. In such systems unprofitable banks would voluntarily wind up their affairs without waiting for insolvency. Bank owners had no incentive to pursue double-or-nothing strategies even as the bank's net worth became negative, because further losses in net worth continued to fall entirely on the shareholders, rather than on depositors or on a deposit guarantee agency. It may be that unlimited shareholder liability, or even extended liability, is not generally the optimal risk-sharing arrangement between shareholders and depositors. That is a question financial markets can resolve in the absence of subsidies and legal restrictions. It is not obvious that extended liability is incompatible with tradable shares, though for obvious reasons shareholders whose own exposure depends on the wealth of their coshareholders might want shares to carry covenants regarding ownership qualifications.[11]

In the absence of government deposit guarantees, a *caveat emptor* policy prevails. With entry free into both limited-liability and extended-liability banking, depositors who choose limited-liability banks are choosing freely to expose themselves to default risk, in exchange for whatever comparative benefits limited-liability banks can offer them. The usual objections to such a policy are (1) that depositors would attempt to free-ride on one another's efforts to monitor the bank, so that too little monitoring would take place; and (2) that depositors would run on suspect banks, setting off contagious banking panics.

The first objection is not really specific to banking. Quality-assurance problems of this sort are generally handled by certification agencies. In banking, a private clearinghouse association has historically been the agency acting to certify the solvency and liquidity of its member banks, primarily because each member bank (who accepts the liabilities of its fellow members daily) has a strong interest in receiving such quality assurances (Timberlake 1984; White 1992, ch. 2).

The second objection is undercut by the historical evidence that a run on a suspect bank is not generally contagious. In the absence of legal restrictions that weaken banks in similar ways, bank failures do not occur in droves, and so depositors do not rationally infer from one bank's difficulties that all others are about to default. No contagions are recorded in Canadian or Scottish banking history, where banks were free to branch nationwide and to capitalize adequately. Even in the United States there is little evidence (outside the exceptional years of 1929–33) of runs spreading generally from insolvent to solvent banks (Kaufman 1988, 566–71; Schwartz 1988, 591–93).

Depositors fleeing suspect banks generally redeposit their funds in sound banks. Such movements were occurring in the early 1930s, and one suspects that the private interest of weak banks in opposing such a "flight into quality" explains why small banks enthusiastically supported the formation of the FDIC, while many large banks opposed it. If so, the same sort of interest today would oppose "coinsurance" proposals (limiting deposit guarantees to, say, 90% of deposits). Weak banks (a category that today includes many of the largest banks as well as the smallest U.S. banks) may fear that coinsurance might deliver on its advocates' claims: it might reimpose market discipline.

Proposals to limit deposit guarantees to "narrow banks" (Litan 1987) are a step toward the goal of an undistorted financial system provided that banks are free to issue explicitly and credibly unguaranteed accounts on whatever terms informed customers find agreeable. A number of options are open to banks to make their accounts run-resistant or even run-proof. Deposit contracts could contain notice-of-withdrawal clauses. Checking accounts could be linked to money-market mutual funds, equity rather than debt claims. Capital adequacy assurances, or even extended shareholder liability, could be offered. Some sort of private deposit insurance might be feasible.

Assuring that the best sorts of financial contracts win out on a level playing field requires eliminating the discriminatory practices in the current operation of the clearing and settlement system (e.g., the exclusion of money-market funds from direct use of the Fedwire, and the unpriced guarantee of interbank payments made by wire). Ideally the payments system would be entirely privatized.

The case for government deposit guarantees in a deregulated environment is not persuasive. Any government deposit guarantees that remain in this environment must at a minimum be self-financing. If the guarantee system cannot cover its costs, it is hard to defend its efficiency. If the deposits of banks (however narrow) are provided with government guarantees at rates subsidized by general taxation, there are inadequate incentives for savers to seek efficient alternative intermediary forms (such as mutual funds). In the context of proposals currently on the table, this means that if making the Bank Insurance Fund self-financing by raising FDIC assessments on banks makes the banking industry shrink that much faster, so be it.

Notes

1. Bill Atkinson and Robert M. Garsson, "Bank Fund Loss Put at $3 Billion," *American Banker* (28 September 1990): 2; Catherine Yang, "The FDIC Keeps Digging a Deeper Hole," *Business Week* (15 July 1991): 123.

   The net loss projections for 1991–92 are derived following the FDIC's method as reported by Barbara A. Rehm, "Capital Issue: What Price the BIF Recap?" *American Banker* (4 April 1991), using the FDIC's mid-1991 bank failure predictions reported by Peter Stone, "The Balance Sheet on Banking Reform," *Atlanta Journal-Constitution* (22 September 1991): H1. The FDIC predicted that 1991–92 would see the failure of 340–400 banks with $140–200 billion in assets. About 15% of those assets are expected to be unrecoverable, and half to sell for 15–20% below book, implying gross losses of $31.5 to $50 billion. Premium income, at the rate of 23 cents per $100 of insured deposits, is projected at $12.4 billion. Projected net losses are therefore $19.1 to $37.6 billion.
2. Atkinson and Garsson, op. cit.; Yang, op. cit.
3. Barbara A. Rehm, "FDIC Is Said to Forecast $4 Billion Deficit by 1993," *American Banker* (25 January 1991): 1; Idem, "FDIC Deficit Will Be Manageable, Congressional Budget Office Says," *American Banker* (30 January 1991): 13; Idem, "Bankers to Discuss FDIC Fund Plan: Liquidity, Equity Pool, Early Intervention Are Goals," *American Banker* (7 February 1991): 2; Stephen Labaton, "U.S. Seeks Much Bigger Amount to Shore Up Bank Deposit Fund," *New York Times* (22 March 1991): A1.
4. Bill Atkinson, "Seidman's Views on Fund: Pessimistic or Even Worse," *American Banker* (28 June 1991): 2; Stone, op. cit.
5. Brett Duval Fromson, "Will the FDIC Run Out of Money?" *Fortune* (8 October 1990): 119–26; "Deposit Insurance: Required, but Not Desired," *Economist* (22 December 1990): 95; "Veribanc Study Finds FDIC Insolvent," *Journal of Accountancy* (July 1991): 28–29; Yang, op. cit.
6. "Deposit Insurance," op. cit.: 94.
7. Barth, Brumbaugh, and Litan (1990, 34–40) computed "implied market capital when the [put option] value of deposit insurance is stripped away" for sixty-three of the nation's largest banks. They found the Bank

of New England insolvent (as of June 1990) by this criterion. Three other banks were on the edge (insolvent when the option value estimate is higher due to greater assumed forbearance, barely solvent otherwise): Midlantic (NJ), Southeast Banking Corp. (Miami), and Valley National (Phoenix). Bank regulators have forced Midlantic to stop paying out dividends, and in January 1991 its chairman announced his resignation (*American Banker*, 25 January 1991, 1–2).

8. The phrase in quotation marks is due to Rothbard (1972).
9. It is appropriate to average annual figures, rather than looking only at the end years, because the reported net income varies greatly year to year depending on when banks choose to make loan loss provisions. Reported net income was way down in 1987 because the large banks chose en masse to make provisions in that year for losses on LDC loans.
10. In the three years 1980–82 the FSLIC resolved a total of 361 insolvencies. In the previous five years they had resolved only forty-one (Kane 1989, 26, table 2–1; compare Brumbaugh 1988, 11, table 1–2, where the 1980–82 total is 368.
11. Perhaps such covenants are all Woodward (1988, 689) has in mind when she writes that "*publicly* traded shares and extended liability are not compatible" (emphasis added). She is quite right to argue against legally precluding limited liability for banking firms, which I am not suggesting. Nor am I motivated, as are those she criticizes, by the desire to protect a government deposit guarantee agency.

References

Barth, James R.; Brumbaugh, R. Dan, Jr.; and Litan, Robert E. *The Banking Industry in Turmoil: A Report on the Condition of the U.S. Banking Industry and the Bank Insurance Fund*. Washington: U.S. Government Printing Office, 1990.

Benston, George J., and Kaufman, George G. "Risks and Failures in Banking: Overview, History, and Evaluation." In George G. Kaufman and Roger C. Kormendi, eds., *Deregulating Financial Services: Public Policy in Flux*. Cambridge: Ballinger, 1986.

Brumbaugh, R. Dan, Jr. *Thrifts under Seige: Restoring Order to American Banking*. Cambridge: Ballinger, 1988.

Byron, Christopher. "The Bad-News Banks." *New York* (8 October 1990): 16–21.

Cole, Rebel A.; McKenzie, Joseph A.; and White, Lawrence J. "The Causes and Costs of Thrift Institution Failures: A Structure-Behavior-Outcomes Approach." Federal Reserve Bank of Dallas working paper (December 1990).

Duca, John V., and McLaughlin, Mary M. "Developments Affecting the

Profitability of Commercial Banks." *Federal Reserve Bulletin* (July 1990): 477–99.

Eisenbeis, Robert A. "Restructuring Banking." *Challenge* (January-February 1990): 18–21.

England, Catherine. "Judging the 1991 Reform Effort: Do U.S. Banks Have a Future?" Cato Institute *Policy Analysis* (12 March 1991).

Farrell, Christopher. "Will Banks Drag the Economy Down? Yes: We May Be in for a 'Contained Depression.' " *Business Week* (21 January 1991): 28–29.

FDIC Quarterly Banking Profile (Third Quarter 1990).

———. (Second Quarter 1991).

Federal Reserve Bank of New York. *Recent Trends in Commercial Bank Profitability: A Staff Study.* New York: Federal Reserve Bank of New York, 1986.

Fromson, Brett Duval. "Will the FDIC Run Out of Money?" *Fortune* (8 October 1990): 119–26.

Kane, Edward J. *The Gathering Crisis in Federal Deposit Insurance.* Cambridge: MIT Press, 1985.

———. *The S&L Insurance Mess: How Did It Happen?* Washington, DC: Urban Institute Press, 1989.

Kaufman, George G. "Bank Runs: Causes, Benefits, and Costs." *Cato Journal* 7 (Winter 1988): 559–87.

Kohn, Meir. *Money, Banking, and Financial Markets.* Chicago: Dryden, 1991.

Litan, Robert E. *What Should Banks Do?* Washington, DC: Brookings Institution, 1987.

Lucas, Robert E., Jr. *Studies in Business Cycle Theory.* Cambridge: MIT Press, 1981.

Mandel, Michael J. "Will Banks Drag the Economy Down? No: Banks Aren't as Critical to the Economy Now." *Business Week* (21 January 1991): 29–30.

O'Driscoll, Gerald P., Jr. "Deposit Insurance in Theory and Practice." *Cato Journal* 7 (Winter 1988): 661–75.

Rosenthal, James A., and Ocampo, Juan M. *Securitization of Credit: Inside the New Technology of Finance.* New York: Wiley, 1988.

Rothbard, Murray N. *America's Great Depression.* Los Angeles: Nash, 1972.

Salsman, Richard. *Breaking the Banks: Central Banking Problems and Free Banking Solutions.* Great Barrington, MA: American Institute for Economic Research, 1990.

Schwartz, Anna J. "Bank Runs and Deposit Insurance Reform." *Cato Journal* 7 (Winter 1988): 589–94.

Short, Genie D., and Robinson, Kenneth J. "Deposit Insurance Reform in the Post-FIRREA Environment: Lessons from the Texas Deposit Market." Federal Reserve Bank of Dallas working paper (December 1990).

Timberlake, Richard H. "The Central Banking Role of Clearinghouse Associations." *Journal of Money, Credit, and Banking* 16 (February 1984): 1–15.

White, Lawrence H. *The Theory of Monetary Institutions*. Book manuscript in progress, 1992.

Woodward, Susan. "A Transaction Cost Analysis of Banking Activity and Deposit Insurance." *Cato Journal* 7 (Winter 1988): 683–99.

2

Public-Sector Deficits and Private-Sector Performance

Roger W. Garrison

I. Introduction

The detrimental effects of public-sector deficits on private-sector performance can be established without reference to determinate and empirically demonstrable effects of budgetary deficits on interest rates, inflation rates, or exchange rates. The arguments in this chapter, in fact, depend upon the absence of reliable predictions concerning such specific effects. The certainty that deficits must somehow be accommodated, coupled with the uncertainty about just how they will be accommodated, can result in a significant degradation of economic performance in the private sector. The word "performance" is used here and throughout the chapter in place of the more narrowly conceived "efficiency." The intent is to focus attention on the economy's performance as affected by the quality and compatibility of entrepreneurial decisions rather than on some comparative-static allocational efficiency as might be brought about by entrepreneurs who face no uncertainty. Unforeseeable changes in the method of accommodating the federal deficit, which can account for extensive discoordination among private borrowers, can, in turn, help to account for the declining rate of return (measured net of loan-loss provisions) on the loan portfolios of commercial banks.

If all deficit-induced uncertainties are assumed away—including the uncertainties about how and when taxes will be raised to service and retire the resulting debt—then taxing and borrowing can be thought of as economically equivalent methods of public finance. Under conditions of certainty, the issue of *how* government is financed is a trivial one in comparison to the issue of how *much* government is financed. The actual uncertainties inherent in deficit finance, however, distinguish borrowing from taxing and establish strict limits to the application of the Ricardian Equivalence Theorem.[1] Arguments detailing these uncertainties turn on the distinction between a well-known tax code, on which private borrowers and other market participants can base their planning, and some unspecified and ever-changeable means of deficit accommodation, against which there may be no effective hedge.

Heavy reliance by the government on credit markets, then, can impose a burden on the private sector and especially on the banking industry far in excess of the alternative burden associated with taxes collected in accordance with a well-known tax code. The case for taxes over deficits as a means of minimizing the adverse effects of fiscal policy parallels in large measure the case for rules over discretion as a means of minimizing the adverse effects of monetary policy. Accordingly, for a given level of government spending, a budget in balance or in near-balance is strongly preferable to one dramatically out of balance. Establishing the basis for and the nature of this borrowing/taxing nonequivalence is the purpose of the present chapter.

Section 2 employs conventional macroeconomic accounting to identify the possible effects of a budgetary imbalance. Section 3 considers the relevant policy choices and identifies the range of consequences associated with each choice. The macroeconomic accounting allows for an interpretation, in section 4, of recent empirical literature on the effects of budgetary deficits. Section 5 catalogues the proximate consequences of the deficit-induced uncertainties, which derive from the unique features of federal government debt. An historical perspective is provided in section 6 to justify the focus on deficit-induced uncertainties. Section 7 identifies the ultimate consequences of deficit spending in terms of the economy's standard of living, and section 8 concludes with some implications for policy.

II. A Macroeconomic Accounting of Federal Budget Deficits

Consider the federal budget deficit in its relationship to both domestic and foreign components of the private sector. Conventional income-expenditure analysis allows the interconnectedness among the three sectors representing government, domestic investment, and foreign trade to be expressed as a simple summation of differences whose net value is zero:

Eq. 1: $(G - T) + (I - S) + (X - M) = 0$

where G = government expenditures
T = tax revenues
I = investment spending
S = private and corporate saving
X = revenues from exports
M = expenditures on imports

This equation acknowledges one particular constraint that characterizes an economy in macroeconomic equilibrium.[2] Clearly, Equation 1 is satisfied when $G = T$, $I = S$, and $X = M$. That is, the sectoral accounts of the macroeconomy are in balance when government finances its programs with tax revenues, domestic investment is funded by private and corporate saving, and revenues from exports match expenditures on imports.

A balancing of the macroeconomy achieved through a balancing of each sector is, of course, only a special case. In the general case, the macroeconomy is characterized by a balancing of sectoral imbalances. That is, while none of the three separate terms in Equation 1 has a value of zero, the algebraic sum of the terms is constrained by the interconnectedness of the three sectors to be zero. And so long as the government sector is not chronically and dramatically out of balance, the individual imbalances are no cause for concern.

A brief consideration of the relationship between the investment sector $(I - S)$ and the foreign-trade sector $(X - M)$ suggests that balance in all three sectors individually is not to be held up as an ideal. A foreign trade deficit that allows domestic investment to outpace domestic saving may be attributable to favorable economic and political conditions in the home country. Capital may be flowing in from abroad to take advantage of a relatively productive economic environment and to be protected by a relatively stable and unthreatening political regime. Sectoral imbalances rooted in such circumstances, as actually existed in this country throughout most of the last century, are an integral part of the market process and serve to enhance rather than degrade the economy's performance.

Sectoral imbalances that reflect a chronic and dramatic imbalance in the public sector, however, are a different matter. Deficit-induced uncertainties embedded in the offsetting imbalances in the investment and foreign-trade sectors can inhibit market processes and degrade economic performance. These uncertainties and resulting inhibitions, in fact, are central to the argument for a balance or near-balance in the federal budget. And while it is recognized that the offsetting imbalances in the investment and foreign-trade sectors attributable to a budgetary deficit should be measured relative to the imbalances that would exist in these two sectors if the federal budget were in balance, the arguments to follow assume for the convenience of exposition that except for the consequences of the budgetary imbalance, the other two sectors would be individually in balance.

Currently, the federal government is dramatically outspending its tax revenues. This budgetary imbalance implies, in accordance with Equation 1, some combination of offsetting imbalances in the investment and foreign-trade sectors. Domestic saving may be diverted away from private credit markets and into the federal treasury; revenues received by our trading partners may be lent to the federal government rather than spent on exportable goods. The former effect constitutes a crowding out of domestic investment; the latter constitutes a foreign-trade deficit.

For an arithmetic example, a year in which the federal budget deficit (G − T) is $200 billion must also be characterized by imbalances in the other two sectors that sum to a negative $200 billion. If the foreign-trade deficit (M − X) is, say, $160 billion, then the investment sector must be experiencing a crowding out (S − I) in the amount of $40 billion. Equation 1 can be rearranged as Equation 1a and read using this conventional macroeconomic terminology:

Eq. 1(a): $(G - T) = (S - I) + (M - X)$
The federal budget deficit
= crowding out
+ the foreign-trade deficit.

The sectoral imbalances in the form of crowding out and the foreign trade deficit represent the proximate consequences of the budgetary imbalance. The ultimate consequence (to be discussed in section 7) is a lower standard of living as measured by forced reductions in consumer spending. Further, it will be argued that the inherent uncertainties that characterize the proximate consequences of a budgetary imbalance, which manifest themselves as greater riskiness in the private sector and a lower rate of return (net of loan-loss provisions) in the banking industry, add substantially to the severity of the ultimate consequences.

The policy perspective to follow in section 3 is derived directly from the income-expenditure equation and macroeconomic accounting identities. No particular behavioral equations describing the behavior of market participants are postulated, and hence no particular structural relationships that might give determinacy to the macroeconomic magnitudes represented in Equations 1 and 1(a) are implied. The leap from macroeconomic accounting to policy perspective is intended, in fact, to highlight the structural indeterminacies and uncertainties that are implied by a chronic and dramatic budgetary imbalance.[3]

III. Deficits from a Policy Perspective

Policy choice has a direct effect on the left-hand side of Equation 1; it influences the right-hand side as the market responds to current policy actions and to anticipations of future policy actions. If current policy choices have the government's outlay of funds running dramatically ahead of its intake of funds, then there are further choices to be made. The act of borrowing, by its very nature, requires some subsequent action by the fiscal—and possibly the monetary—authorities.[4] For a given level of government spending, the actual menu of policy choice in the face of a budgetary deficit consists of a short list of easily identifiable options.

1. The fiscal authority can continue to borrow in domestic and foreign credit markets.
2. The monetary authority can monetize the deficits, replacing privately saved money with publicly printed money.
3. The legislature can increase the level of taxation.

Historically, piecemeal fiscal and monetary policy is more accurately described in terms of a buffet rather than a menu: The government typically opts for some combination of these menu items.

The relationship between policy (both fiscal and monetary) and its short-run consequences (for the investment and foreign-trade sectors of the economy) is wholly determinate in aggregate terms but hopelessly indeterminate in sectoral terms. That is, private credit markets, both domestic and foreign, and the monetary authority—in some combination—accommodate the budget deficit, which is offset—again, in some combination—by crowding out and the foreign-trade deficit. But the relationships between the individual components of the policy mix and the effects in the individual sectors are not so easily stipulated. Nor is there any reason to believe that these relationships, whatever they currently are, hold over time and particularly from one political regime to the next.

Further, the policy mix itself is largely unpredictable. We can note—after the fact—something about the general fiscal strategy characterizing particular periods. During the Carter administration, for instance, debt was monetized; during the Reagan administration, debt was sold abroad. But we cannot say that federal budget deficits are accommodated by the monetary authority in some systematic or predictable way. And we cannot say what portion of the borrowing not facilitated by money creation will draw funds from foreign as opposed to domestic sources. The particular policy mix and the resulting mix of consequences depend critically upon unique political factors and upon diverse and changing beliefs about the current policy regime and expectations about subsequent regimes.

IV. Empirical Studies and Their Collective Significance

The empirical literature on the effects of the federal budget deficits is replete with correlations and so-called causality tests that focus on a single component of the policy mix or on a single sector of the economy. Does deficit spending lead to an increase in the monetary base? Are domestic interest rates affected by government borrowing? Do our trading partners supply the credit demanded by the U.S. Treasury? Is there any evidence of crowding out? For each specific question asked, empirical evidence of any such systematic relationship is almost uniformly weak and mixed.[5]

The implication of any one empirical study is commonly taken to be that worry about the deficit is misplaced; the implication of the studies considered collectively is taken to be that the worries—and certainly the hysteria—about the budgetary deficit are largely if not wholly baseless. This reading of the empirical literature is exemplified in Paul Craig Roberts's explanation of "Why the Deficit Hysteria Is Unjustified" (1987). The macroeconomic accounting of the deficit and its consequences argue against downplaying the deficit problem on the basis of weak and mixed empirical findings. In a more enlightened—though less comforting—interpretation of those same empirical studies, the absence of any such strong correlations is the very basis for worry about persistently large deficits.

The nature of the problem from the perspective of a typical business firm can be illustrated in terms of a simple shell game. Imagine that three shells, one of which conceals a pea, have been shuffled about by a seasoned gamester. Some player is then enticed to choose a shell. If the pea is under the chosen shell, the player suffers a substantial loss. The pea will not appear in predictable fashion from under any given shell. The absence of such predictability, of course, does not imply that there is no reason to worry about the pea. Quite to the contrary, the uncertainty about where the pea is, where it might appear next, and how to avoid it is the crux of the matter. Whatever the potential rewards for playing this shell game may be, the more substantial the losses associated with the pea's appearance, the greater is the reluctance to play the game.

When the federal government's deficit is in the twelve-digit range, private business firms are faced with highly uncertain market conditions. Each firm must choose a market strategy, and any firm that chooses the wrong strategy will suffer losses accordingly. A firm in the business of cutting and exporting timber, for example, may choose to maintain or even increase its capacity in anticipation of a reduced willingness on the part of our trading partners to buy U.S. government debt and hence of generally strengthened export markets. If this anticipation fails to become a reality, the firm will suffer a substantial loss. An industrial developer, for another example, who assumes that foreigners will continue to buy U.S. government debt, may undertake long-term projects counting on continued credit at or near current rates of interest. The assumption, though, may turn out to be wrong. The Treasury may have to begin competing for domestic savings, in which case interest rates rise and the developer suffers a substantial loss.

The economy, of course, is far more complex than a shell game. In reality each entrepreneur (or proprietor or corporate planner) must cope with what might be called multitier uncertainty. First, there is the uncertainty that characterizes any decentralized market economy. The absence of "perfect knowledge" and of "known probability distributions" pertaining to product demand, resource availabilities, and technological possibilities is what makes the real-world market process different from textbook exercises. Each entrepreneur must act on the basis of his or her judgment about these things as well as his or her judgment about the likely actions of other entrepreneurs.

Second, there is the uncertainty that is associated with each choice available to the fiscal and monetary authorities for accommodating the budgetary deficit. (1) Continued recourse to private credit markets requires that private planning agents guess about the government's particular source of loanable funds. If our trading partners continue to supply those funds, then export markets will be weak; if there is an increased reluctance on the part of foreign savers or of foreign central banks to extend credit to the U.S. Treasury, then domestic interest rates will be high. (2) Debt monetization means a general price inflation during which there are transitional disturbances to real interest rates and exchange rates as well as increased uncertainties about the significance of any individual price change. Burdening the normal market process with the additional task of adjusting to a growing money supply means that price signals involve ambiguities. In general, nominal interest rates and exchange rates as well as product and factor prices become less reliable guides to entrepreneurial action. (3) A credible commitment by the fiscal authority to reduce or eliminate the deficit by increasing taxes leaves private planning agents to guess about the particulars of the new tax code. Possibilities include income taxes, corporate-profit taxes, value-added taxes, sales taxes, and sumptuary taxes. Each type of tax has its own effect on the plans of private planning agents.[6]

Third, the uncertainties associated with each policy choice are compounded by the uncertainty about which choice or which combination of choices will actually be made. That is, there is uncertainty about the nature of the uncertainty that will characterize market conditions during the planning period. Will there be continued reliance on credit markets? Will there be debt monetization? Will there be new taxes? It is often taken for granted in the writings of modern political economists that public debt gets inflated away. Arguably, if this particular solution to the current problem of fiscal imbalance were a certainty, the high level of indebtedness would be less haunting than it actually is. Statistical studies showing that debt is not *always* monetized (or that domestic interest rates do not *always* rise when the treasury's demand for credit increases, or that the foreign-trade deficit does not *always* move in lockstep with the federal budget deficit) do not lessen our concern about government borrowing; they simply reinforce the notion that the uncertainty about the particulars of deficit accommodation is the essence of the problem.

A fourth tier of uncertainty derives from the general interconnectedness of markets. Uncertainties that are inherent in the market process consist in part—as mentioned above—of entrepreneurial judgments about the actions of other entrepreneurs. In an era of deficit finance, these judgments are more difficult to make. For each entrepreneur, then, uncertainties already identified are exacerbated by uncertainties about how other entrepreneurs will attempt to hedge or exploit this fiscal imbalance in making their own plans.

The deficit-induced multitier uncertainties faced by commercial and industrial planners translate directly into problems for the banking industry. The banks' borrowers must make guesses about future market conditions as affected by deficit accommodation. And under plausible circumstances, if they guess wrong, they lose big. Managers of the banks' loan portfolios must make judgments about the abilities of their borrowers to anticipate deficit-related changes in market conditions as well as judgments about their more narrowly conceived creditworthiness. If a bank makes loans on the basis of its *own* guess about the future course of deficit accommodation, then it subjects itself to dramatic losses, should the guess prove wrong; if it makes loans on the basis of a diversity of guesses, then it must accept the lower net rate of return implied by such hedging.

V. Market Manifestations of Deficit-Induced Uncertainties

Uncertainty, by its very nature, is difficult to assess. And the fact that there is inherent uncertainty in the market process compounds the problem of assessing the (additional) uncertainty attributable to budgetary deficits. Under conditions of perfect knowledge and perfect foresight, deficit-financed programs in the amount of $200 billion would impose costs on society of exactly $200 billion in terms of foregone alternatives. This first approximation of the social costs is based squarely on the Ricardian Equivalence Theorem and assumes that the burden of the debt is borne by individuals in society in some economically efficient way. The actual uncertainty that surrounds the deficit and its possible effect on market conditions obscures the social costs, virtually assuring that those costs, though less clearly perceived, are actually greater. The several considerations below suggest that added social costs in the form of discoordination, economic crises, risk externalities, and loan-market perversities are substantial.

1. *Deficits discoordinate.* A market system facilitates the coordination of plans among a multitude of market participants. A fully coordinated set of plans would require each market participant to have the same perception of the relevant market conditions. Differences in perception lead to arbitrage and speculation, which, in turn, reduce such differences. At the very least, differences in perceptions based on differences in guesses about how the budget deficit will be accommodated put an additional burden on the market process. A borrower who believes that the government will soon begin to monetize its debt is borrowing at a relatively low real rate of interest (as perceived by the borrower); a lender who believes that the government will continue to sell its debt abroad is receiving a relatively high real rate (as perceived by the lender).

Such differences in perception can persist for a substantial period of time. While disparate plans based on the different perceptions necessarily imply disequilibrium and discoordination, there may be nothing in the nature of the government's fiscal process that eliminates in a timely manner the differences in perception. To the contrary, with each period in which a high budgetary deficit is matched by a high foreign-trade deficit, both perceptions are likely to be strengthened. The lender perceives that the fiscal pattern he or she anticipated is materializing; the borrower perceives that the inevitable debt monetization is even closer at hand. So long as there are differences in the expectations about how the government will deal with its fiscal imbalance in future periods, the corresponding differences in perceived market conditions will result in a greater degree of discoordination among market participants than would otherwise exist.

2. *Deficits destabilize.* Whole industries can function for extended periods of time without any clear manifestation of the deficit-induced discoordination that may exist within or among them. Plans of individual firms may be based on some broadly—though not deeply—held belief about the future course of fiscal policy. But such underlying belief, precisely because it is characterized by breadth but not depth, is subject to dramatic change as a result of undramatic events.

Suppose that market conditions in a particular industry reflect a belief that massive debt monetization accompanied by double-digit inflation will characterize the near-to-intermediate future. A series of individually undramatic actions taken by the Federal Reserve may eventually establish the new belief that monetary policy is going to remain tight even in the face of a loose fiscal policy. This shift from one market-ruling belief to another can account for otherwise unexplainable crises, such as the crisis in agriculture in recent years. Individual farmers, accommodated by the banking industry, prepared to benefit from the expected debt monetization by incurring heavy debts of their own and then faced heavy losses in capital and land values when the Federal Reserve did not turn those expectations into reality.

In similar fashion, deficit-induced uncertainty can affect capital markets on an economy-wide basis. Market conditions on Wall Street near the peak of the 1980s' bull market, for instance, reflected a belief that the Reagan administration would go the distance on funds borrowed abroad. Mounting U.S. indebtedness and increased reluctance on the part of our trading partners to lend still more funds to the U.S. Treasury eventually tipped the balance toward a new belief that the Federal Reserve would be forced to loosen its monetary policy in order to accommodate the Treasury. But actions taken by the Federal Reserve signaling continuing monetary discipline shattered this new belief, leaving no one particular belief in its place.

Conflicting hints about the course of fiscal and monetary policy caused the shifting from one broadly but not deeply held belief to another to be preempted by a disintegration of all such beliefs. Uncertainty in a more salient form began to dominate the market for equity shares, and a scramble for liquidity resulted in a sharp fall in stock prices. Changing market conditions as a result of deficit-induced uncertainties is a very plausible basis for explaining the volatility of the stock market during the first three quarters of 1987 and the unprecedented crash in October of that year.

John Maynard Keynes (1964, 153–58) argued that such stock-market volatility is inherent in the nature of the market. Dramatic and unpredictable changes in business psychology turn the securities market into "a game of Snap, Old Maid, or Musical Chairs." Interpreters of Keynes who focus on these aspects of his *General Theory* compare the pattern of asset prices to the pattern of cut glass in a kaleidoscope and dwell on the inherent unknowability of future patterns (Shackle 1974). It is possible to reject this Keynesian vision as applied to a decentralized market economy per se but to accept some version of it in the context of persistently large federal budget deficits. There is some irony, it might be noted, in the idea that deficit spending, which was recommended by so many of Keynes's followers, can cause asset markets to behave precisely in accordance with Keynes's vision of them.

3. *Large deficits externalize risk.* The risks associated with private debt are borne primarily by the individuals who hold the corresponding private securities; the risks created by public debt are *not* borne primarily by the individuals who hold government securities. The risks, of course, are not simply shunted into the ocean or otherwise eliminated by the fiscal authority. Rather, the federal government's powers to tax and to create money provide security to the debt holder by shifting the associated risks away from him or her and onto the citizenry as a whole. The likelihood of the government's defaulting on its debt in the conventional sense is nil, but the likelihood of its defaulting in some other way is all but inevitable. It may partially default by inflating away the real value of outstanding debt. It may default on its promise not to raise taxes. It may default on its commitments to pay retirement or other benefits to government employees and participants in social programs. But default in any of these forms does not impinge directly or exclusively on the holders of government debt; it impinges instead on the wealth holders in general or on the taxpayers or on the beneficiaries of government retirement or social programs. The economic inefficiency in the form of such externalities means that each dollar of deficit spending has a social cost in excess of a dollar.

4. *Large deficits facilitate larger deficits.* The dynamics of increasing indebtedness that work to curb the excesses of private borrowers and even of state and municipal borrowers work to magnify the excesses of the federal fiscal authority. Most borrowers experience an increased difficulty in acquiring additional funds as their level of indebtedness increases. This increased difficulty is a simple reflection of an increased likelihood of default. Thus, a borrower already heavily in debt must pay a substantial default-risk premium for additional loans. And this high cost of borrowing provides an incentive to reduce the level of indebtedness.

The corresponding loan-market dynamics that apply to borrowing by the U.S. Treasury are, at least with respect to domestic savers, precisely opposite to those just mentioned. This perversity is attributable to the special sense in which loans to the federal government are risk free and to the effects of government borrowing on the riskiness of loans to the private sector. Here, a distinction between domestic and foreign buyers of U.S. debt must be maintained. A deficit-induced adjustment in foreign-exchange rates can impose costs more directly on foreign lenders than on domestic lenders. It is this directness, in fact, that explains why foreign lenders are more concerned about the U.S. budget deficit than are domestic buyers of those same Treasury bills.

The federal government's ability to tax distinguishes it from borrowers in the private sector; its ability to create money distinguishes it from state and municipal borrowers. Given this unique status of the federal government, default in the conventional sense is institutionally precluded. There is no default risk in the judgment of the federal government's creditors; there is no default-risk premium in the discounting of Treasury bills.

But while large deficits do not increase the likelihood that the government will default (again, in the conventional sense), they do increase the likelihood of dramatic losses and possibly default in the private sector by adding substantially, as spelled out above, to the uncertainty in the marketplace. As the risk of severe losses and of default grow in the judgment of private creditors, corporate stocks and bonds—and even municipal bonds—become less attractive in comparison to securities issued by the federal government. Perversely, domestic savers buy Treasury bills in order to protect themselves from the uncertainties that are created by the government's issuing of so many Treasury bills.[7]

When the federal government is engaged heavily in deficit finance, it enjoys, in effect, a negative risk premium on further debt issue. That is, the more overextended the U.S. Treasury becomes, the *less* risky its debt becomes relative to private-sector debt. The relatively low and falling cost of borrowing encourages the government to borrow still more. The U.S. Treasury behaves as if it were facing an increasingly elastic and—in the extreme—a negatively sloped long-run supply of loanable funds.

VI. A Historical Perspective

The macroeconomic accounting perspective on budgetary deficits and the attention to deficit-induced uncertainty in the private sector warn against any historical view that focuses too narrowly on interest rates, inflation rates, or exchange rates—or too broadly, say, on this country's gross national product or on total borrowing of the Western world. Public borrowers confront, in the first instance, private savers; the relevant focus for historical analysis is the market for loanable funds. How much is the government borrowing relative to the total amount of funds available for lending? If this ratio of government borrowing to private and corporate saving were so small that the U.S. Treasury is just one among many borrowers in line at the credit window, then there would be no deficit-induced uncertainty of any great consequence. But so long as this ratio is sufficiently large, such that the Treasury must be considered a Big Player in the credit market, then uncertainty about how the government's demand for credit will be accommodated can heavily influence decisions in the private sector.[8]

Although it may seem obvious that a historical treatment should relate the government's demand for credit to the market's supply of credit, attention to the deficit-to-saving ratio is relatively uncommon. More common is a reporting of the ratio of deficit spending to total government spending or the ratio of deficit spending to the gross national product. While these ratios may be rhetorically effective, if the objective is to make a twelve-digit deficit look small, they are relatively weak proxies for the burden on the private sector in the form of deficit-induced uncertainties.

Another increasingly common way of putting the budgetary deficit into historical perspective is to redefine the deficit as the change in the real value of outstanding debt. In this accounting, the consequences of conventionally defined deficits are offset by the debt-eroding inflation that results from actual or anticipated debt monetization. If the government has an outstanding debt in the thirteen-digit range, then double-digit inflation can wholly negate a twelve-digit, conventionally defined deficit. The budget can be declared to be in balance or even in surplus while the Treasury continues to make heavy demands on credit markets.[9]

The change in the real value of outstanding debt may be the relevant magnitude in some contexts. It is relevant, for instance, in arguments that link deficits to changes in perceived net wealth, which, in turn, are linked to spending propensities. But in the context of uncertainties attributable to deficit finance, debt erosion is not an offsetting factor. Rather, the heavy demands on credit markets and the—actual or potential—debt monetization, which fuels the inflation that erodes the debt, are compounding, not counteracting, aspects of the deficit problem.

The accompanying table and bar chart show budget deficits, pri-

Figure 2.1

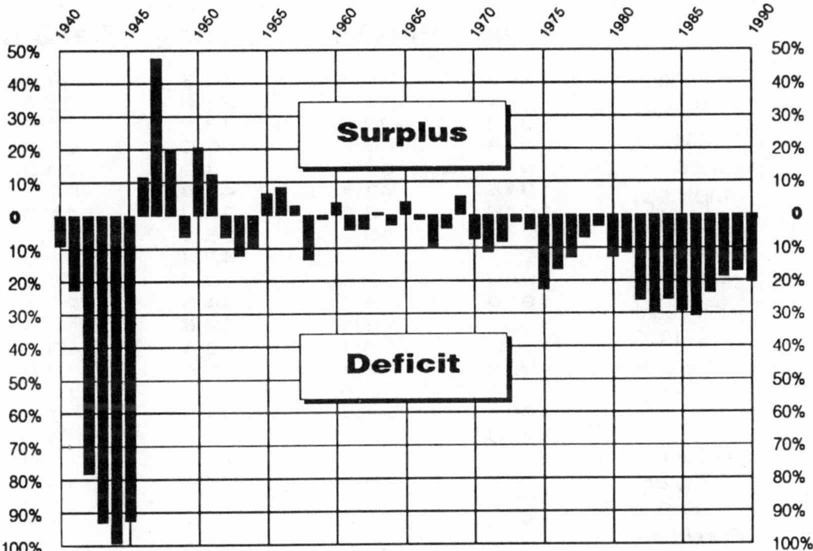

The Federal Budget surplus or deficit as a percentage of private and corporate saving for 1940 through 1990

vate and corporate saving, and the deficit-to-saving ratio for the years 1940 through 1990. Clearly, the ratios for the mid-1970s and beyond are in a categorically different range of values in comparison to the earlier postwar years. A corresponding difference in the nature of the uncertainty faced by the private sector is a plausible basis for a substantial degradation of economic performance. Arguments made in this chapter that the recent budgetary deficits have been substantial enough to increase the degree of discoordination and decrease the stability of asset markets are consistent with the quantitative record.

The current level of budgetary deficits are sometimes downplayed by comparing them to the substantially larger deficits associated with World War II. Whether the deficit is expressed as a proportion of gross national product, of total government spending, or even of private and corporate saving, the ostensive comparison of deficits now to deficits then suggests that the problems posed by the

Table 2.1

Federal Budget deficits (and surpluses) in comparison to corporate and private savings for the years 1940 through 1990

Economic Report of the President

Washington D.C. February 1991, page 318.

Year	Def-(Sur+)	Saving	Def/Sav
1940	**-1.3**	**14.3**	**-9.1**
1941	-5.1	22.6	-22.6
1942	-33.1	42.3	-78.3
1943	-46.6	50.0	-93.2
1944	-54.5	54.9	-99.3
1945	**-42.1**	**45.4**	**-92.7**
1946	3.5	30.3	11.6
1947	13.4	28.1	47.7
1948	8.3	42.4	19.6
1949	-2.6	39.9	-6.5
1950	**9.2**	**44.5**	**20.7**
1951	6.5	52.6	12.4
1952	-3.7	56.1	-6.6
1953	-7.1	58.0	-12.2
1954	-6.0	58.8	-10.2
1955	**4.4**	**65.2**	**6.7**
1956	6.1	72.1	8.5
1957	2.3	76.1	3.0
1958	-10.3	77.1	-13.4
1959	-1.1	82.1	-1.3
1960	**3.0**	**81.1**	**3.7**
1961	-3.9	86.8	-4.5
1962	-4.2	95.2	-4.4
1963	.3	97.9	.3
1964	-3.3	110.8	-3.0
1965	**.5**	**123.0**	**4.0**
1966	-1.8	131.6	-1.4
1967	-13.2	143.8	-9.8
1868	-6.0	145.7	-4.1
1969	-8.4	148.9	5.6
1970	**-12.4**	**164.5**	**-7.5**
1971	-22.0	190.6	-11.5
1972	-16.8	203.4	-8.2
1973	-5.6	244.0	-2.3
1974	-11.7	254.3	-4.6
1975	**-69.4**	**303.6**	**-22.9**
1976	-53.5	321.4	-16.6
1977	-46.0	354.5	-13.0
1978	-29.3	409.0	-7.1
1979	-16.1	445.8	-3.6
1980	**-61.3**	**478.4**	**-12.8**
1981	-63.8	550.5	-11.6
1982	-145.9	557.1	-26.2
1983	-176.0	592.2	-29.7
1984	-169.6	673.5	-25.9
1985	**-196.9**	**665.3**	**-29.6**
1986	-206.9	669.5	-30.9
1987	-158.2	662.6	-23.9
1988	-141.7	751.3	-18.9
1989	-134.3	779.3	-17.2
1990	**-161.3**	**783.9**	**-20.6**

current budgetary imbalance are minor in comparison to the problems posed by wartime deficits. But the considerations outlined in this chapter suggest otherwise. The problem is not deficits per se, but deficit-induced uncertainties. By the end of the war, entrepreneurs could make their plans on the well-founded expectation that the level of government spending would soon be reduced to a peacetime level and hence that the budget deficit would not figure importantly in performance of the private sector. Thus, there was a high deficit through 1946, but there was little or no deficit-induced uncertainty. By contrast, the well-founded expectation in the current period that the level of government spending will remain high into the foreseeable future causes the current high deficits to be crystalized into a cloud of uncertainty. The arguments in this chapter apply to the 1980s and the 1990s but not to the 1940s.

The focus on deficit-induced uncertainties can also be reconciled with the full history of this country's experience with deficit finance. Summarizing data for the period 1789 to present, Barth et al. (1991, 73) identify the episodes of large federal deficits with the Great Depression, recessions, wars, and the 1980s. The inclusion of the 1980s in this short list has a certain unsettling, if not jarring effect. Deficits play special roles in hard times and during wartime; well-founded predictions that recessions and wars will end carry with them the prediction that deficits will fall. But throughout the last decade, even the certain knowledge about the timing of the end of the 1980s provided no basis for predicting an end to large deficits. Uncertainty about credit-market conditions in the immediate and extended future continues to have its impact in the private sector.

Barth et al., review empirical studies of the effects of deficit finance and acknowledge that the collective evidence of systematic harmful effects on interest rates, exchange rates, and the inflation rate is weak and mixed. And they note the continuing theoretical disagreements among economists on the issue of deficits. The implication they draw for policy seems to follow from the inability of the empirical evidence to resolve the theoretical stalemate: "Faced with uncertain outcomes, many (policy advisors) would argue that it is too risky to adopt a view that deficits do not matter when, in fact, this view may be incorrect" (130). But surely, the relevant uncertainties here are not simply the uncertainties on the part of policy advisors about which view of the deficit is correct. The relevant and more fundamental uncertainties are those deficit-induced uncertainties faced by market participants. Accordingly, the policy implication might well be amended to read as follows: Faced with reasonable certainty that large deficits induce uncertainties in the private sector, policy advisors should argue against them.

VII. The Ultimate Consequences of Deficit Spending

The standard income-expenditure framework adopted in Section 2 obscures one significant imbalance. Equations 1 and 1(a) describe revenues and expenditures net of those associated with the consumer-goods sector. But the effects of excessive government borrowing are not confined to domestic investment and foreign trade. Ultimately, the general level of consumption enjoyed by present income earners will also be reduced. The usual neglect of this effect on consumption derives from the short-run focus of Keynesian macroeconomics and the view that consumption spending depends strictly on current income—and not on the interest rate or on other relative prices.

To account for a deficit-induced change in consumption spending, let C_0 and S_0 represent the levels of consumption and saving that would have been realized but for the government's fiscal policies. The summary term $(S - I)$ can then be divided into the two terms $(S - S_0)$ and $(S_0 - I)$, indicating that the total discrepancy is attributable in part to a decrease in investment and in part to an increase in saving. Replacing the term $(S - S_0)$ with its equivalent $(C_0 - C)$ provides an explicit accounting of the consumer-goods sector.

This difference between C_0 and C can be conceptualized in two ways. For one, the concept of crowding out can be extended to include the consumer-goods sector. Government borrowing and spending takes resources out of the private sector. Crowding out in the investment sector is brought about by higher interest rates that reflect the government's increased bids for credit; crowding out in the consumer-goods sector is brought about by higher prices that reflect the government's increased bids for resources.

Alternatively $(C_0 - C)$ can be seen as a form of "forced saving." The relatively high interest rate and consumer-goods prices—both reflections of the government's fiscal policies—cause income earners to save more than they otherwise would. The two conceptualizations are substantively equivalent; the latter is adopted here for expositional convenience. Equations 1 and 1(a) are modified to allow for forced saving:

Eq. 2: $(G - T) + (C - C_0) + (I - S_0) + (X - M) = 0$
Eq. 2(a): $(G - T) = (C_0 - C) + (S_0 - I) + (M - X)$
The federal budget deficit
= forced saving
+ crowding out
+ the foreign-trade deficit.

The concept of forced savings puts the relationship between government borrowing and private saving in a new light. Some economists (notably Barro 1974 and 1989) have argued that government borrowing causes individuals to save more in order to meet higher tax obligations in the future, and that this effect lessens our concern about government deficits. While we can say on the basis of both introspection and casual observation that increased borrowing is not *fully* matched by increased private saving, the present formulation suggests the increase in saving attributable to government borrowing, the forced saving, is one of the effects to be concerned about. The actual saving rate, spurred by deficit spending, reflects policy choice rather than underlying intertemporal preferences and resource constraints.

The relative strengths of the effects on consumption and on investment depend in a significant way upon the length of the time period to which the macroeconomic accounting equation is applied. For accounting periods that are long in comparison to production periods, reduced investment early in a given period will have time to manifest itself as reduced consumption later in the same period. The longer the run, then, the more fully deficit finance gets reflected in the discrepancy term pertaining to the consumer-goods sector. This is only to say that neither individuals nor collections of them can live indefinitely beyond their means. Maintaining a higher standard of living than can be sustained indefinitely implies accepting a correspondingly lower standard of living sometime in the future. In this perspective, the other two terms in Equation 1(a) characterize the transition from one standard of living to another. The deficit-induced uncertainties and consequent discoordination associated with the transition terms, however, can only add to the magnitude of the inevitable reduction in the standard of living.

VIII. A Summary Perspective

Attention to deficit-induced uncertainties allows for a brief summary of the deficit problem (1) as it relates to the crisis in the banking industry, (2) in the context of strategic as well as analytical considerations, and (3) as it compares to the deficit problem more conventionally conceived.

1. Although the primary focus of this chapter has been on the deficit problem itself, the persistently large deficits of the last several years and the consequent uncertainties about market conditions have undoubtedly contributed to the crisis in the banking industry. I do not suggest that the deficit has played the lead role in the current banking crisis, but rather an important supporting role that has been largely neglected. Other chapters in this volume, as well as an earlier paper of mine (Garrison, Short, and O'Driscoll 1988), have argued that the perversities created by the mispricing of deposit insurance lie at the root of the banking crisis. Because of the deposit-insurance subsidy, banks are led to take on more risk than they otherwise would and, if their capital base suffers sufficient erosion, to pursue shoot-the-moon strategies in their gamble for revival.

As it turns out, then, the deficit problem and the deposit insurance problem are not unrelated.[10] Deficit-induced uncertainties create prime opportunities for banks to pursue shoot-the-moon strategies. For instance, if a bank heavily slants its loan portfolio towards assets that appreciate with and are sensitive to inflation, then it stands to win big if the federal government shifts from a strategy of selling debt abroad to a strategy of debt monetization. But if heavy lending of this sort, such as lending in the areas of land development and commercial real estate, is followed by continued reliance on foreign sales of Treasury debt and continued monetary restraint, the consequences for the banks pursuing this shoot-the-moon strategy will be capital depletion and bankruptcy. The mispricing of deposit insurance and the imbalance in the federal budget may well have contributed both separately and interactively to the current banking crisis.

2. The policy perspective in section 2 as well as the discussion in other sections has taken the current, historically high level of government spending as given. This method of argument is not intended to imply a belief that government spending should not be reduced. Nor does it reflect some judgment made by the author that a reduction is out of the question. It reflects, instead, the judgment that such a reduction constitutes no part of the expectations of entrepreneurs and hence does not figure significantly in the uncertainty attributable to the budgetary deficit.

A balance or near-balance in the government budget is a symptom

—but not the essence—of fiscal responsibility. A balance at high levels of spending and taxing may be more detrimental to the private sector than an imbalance at low levels. But the case against raising taxes, based broadly on a comparison of allocative efficiency of the public sector with that of the private sector, should not blind us to the special problems created by persistently large budget deficits and the uncertainties that they entail.

Nor should these special problems be downplayed because of political factors that link taxing and spending. The argument is that *for a given level of government spending,* taxing is preferable to borrowing. If political considerations all but insure that increased taxes will be accompanied by increased spending rather reduced deficits, then a higher level of taxation would be ineffective, if not counterproductive. A blend of economic and political understanding can provide strong support for balancing the budget through reductions in government spending.

3. The character of deficits as seen by three loosely defined schools of thought has been identified by Charles Schultze (1989) as that of wolves, termites, and pussycats. Wolves threaten imminent disaster; termites eat away at the economy's capital base; pussycats do—and threaten to do—nothing. The uncertainty associated with deficits together with the political link between taxing and spending allows for an addition to the Schultze menagerie. The imagery below is intended to relate borrowing to its alternative of taxing as evaluated by entrepreneurs—or, more broadly, by tax-paying market participants.

We can conceive of the government's fiscal strategy as a cat-and-mouse game in which the cats are federal fiscal agents who are looking to fund their spending programs, and the mice are entrepreneurs or other market participants who are looking out for cats. To hunt for the needed funding, the cats are organized into two groups. Cats in the first group, which is charged with collecting taxes, wear bells around their necks; cats in the second group, which is charged with accommodating the deficit, wear no bells. The mice are fond of neither group, but at least they know where members of the first group are, and they make their own plans accordingly. And even though the second group is smaller than the first, the threat of harm as well as actual harm done by the unbelled cats is relatively large.

The pussycat view of the deficit, identified by Schultze, is that deficits are harmless, or at least no more harmful than taxes: Cats are cats, bells or no bells. The alternative imagery offered here suggests otherwise. Cats are a threat, all the more so if they are not wearing bells. Some mice might well conceive of a scheme to bell the unbelled cats, to reduce deficit spending by raising taxes. But belling cats is itself a risky business and ultimately a counterproductive one if with each newly belled cat another unbelled cat is recruited to look for still more funds.

The cat-and-mouse analogy offered in the spirit of Schultze, like the more serious arguments in earlier sections, maintains a distinction between analytical and strategic issues—between economics and politics. Shading economic analysis with policy predispositions is likely to result in both bad analysis and bad policy. More pointedly, efforts to restore fiscal responsibility in the public sector should be based not on some false hope or on a politically motivated argument that heavy government borrowing is inconsequential but rather on the fullest understanding of the effects of public-sector deficits on private-sector performance.

Notes

The author thanks Jim Barth, Dan Gropper, Gerald O'Driscoll, Parth Shah, and Leland Yeager for their helpful comments and thanks the Mises Institute of Auburn University for its financial support in connection with the presentation of an earlier version of this chapter at the 1991 Southwest Economic Association meetings in San Antonio.

1. The idea that imposing a one-time tax of, say, $100 is equivalent, given an interest rate of 10%, to selling a $100 perpetual bond that is then serviced by an annual tax of $10 is typically attributed to Ricardo. Although Ricardo's treatment of tax and deficit financing clearly recognizes the formal stock/flow equivalence between $100 now and $10 from now on, his discussion focused on the ways that borrowing differs from taxing. See O'Driscoll (1977).
2. Equation 1 follows straightforwardly from (1) the proposition that income, Y, is equal to the expenditures that generate it (expenditures on consumer goods, investment goods, government programs, and net exports): $Y = C + I + G + (X—M)$ and (2) the definition of saving as income net of consumption expenditures and taxes: $S = Y - C - T$. The use of this income-expenditure equality and accounting identity, which serve as bedrock for Keynesian macroeconomics, does not imply the acceptance of Keynesian behavioral relationships, such as the psychological considerations that supposedly govern investment spending,

or the adoption of the Keynesian vision of the market process in which incomes—rather than prices, wage rates, and interest rates—adjust to bring about the equality between total income and total expenditure.

3. Robert Eisner (1991, 90–97) criticizes those who discuss policy on the basis of the accounting identities. In his own treatment of deficits, he bridges the gap between accounting identities and policy prescription by postulating Keynesian behavioral and structural relationships. The fact that these relationships—as well as the alternative relationships postulated by Monetarists, Supply Siders, New Classicists, and others —are a matter of continuing controversy justify the focus in the present chapter on the uncertainties about the consequences of large budgetary deficits.
4. The distinction here between taxing, which has a certain finality about it, and borrowing, which requires some subsequent fiscal and/or monetary action, gives substance to the focus on deficit-induced uncertainties. When the government borrows, market participants are, in effect, continually waiting for policymakers to "drop the other fiscal shoe."
5. For a sampling of such piecemeal studies, see Dewald and Ulan (1989), Dwyer (1982), Evans (1985), Fackler and McMillin (1989), Kormendi (1983), and Niskanen (1988). Barth et al. (1991), present the weak and mixed findings of forty-two different empirical studies in which the effects of the federal debt and deficit on short-term and long-term interest rates are investigated.
6. To the extent that the new deficit-reducing taxes are not fully specified in terms of type, rate, and timing, the uncertainties about the new taxes may be as great as the uncertainties about the deficit. Trial balloons during the Reagan administration that hinted at various tax-reform measures had unsettling effects on Wall Street and drew expressions of fear and worry from the financial community. Administration spokesmen, who evidently did not recognize that the market was reacting to the uncertainties created by the tax-reform proposal, attempted to allay those fears and worries with repeated assurances that the proposal was "written on a word processor"—which meant, of course, that it easily could and probably would be altered. The relevant distinction here is not strictly the taxing/borrowing distinction but rather the distinction between taxes collected in accordance with a well-known tax code and other funds to be raised in yet-to-be-specified ways—which include *new* taxes.
7. Bowles, Ulbrich, and Wallace (1989) believe that government indebtedness and default risk on corporate securities are related *negatively*. Their argument is straightforwardly Keynesian. Expansionary fiscal policy in the form of increased deficit spending stimulates the economy, improving economic conditions generally and thus reducing the risk of

default for business firms. Their empirical support for this negative relationship makes use of annual data from 1959 to 1985 on (1) the spread between *Baa* corporate securities and U.S. Treasury securities and (2) the cyclically adjusted deficit. An examination of the authors' data suggests that their results are sensitive to the cyclical adjustment. For instance, the $146 billion deficit in 1982, a recession year, translates into a low cyclically adjusted deficit, which then gets paired with a high spread between corporate and government securities. A visual inspection of their constructed time series on this spread, however, suggests that it increased from the 1960s to the 1970s and increased again from the 1970s to the 1980s. This time pattern of corporate-government risk differentials mirrors the time pattern of (unadjusted) deficit-to-saving ratio presented in the following section and suggests a positive rather than a negative relationship between government indebetedness and default risk on corporate securities.

8. The relevant distinction here between the U.S. Treasury and others in line at the credit window is one identified by Machlup (1978). The others in line at the credit window have an atomistic composition; the law of large numbers applies; the individual borrowers remain "anonymous"—to use Machlup's own characterization—while the consequences of their collective behavior can be predicted on the basis of economic principles. In contrast, predictions about the actions of the U.S. Treasury, as affected by fiscal and monetary authorities, requires a more "intimate" knowledge—again, Machlup's characterization—of the particular circumstances and particular individuals involved. The term "Big Player" in this context was introduced by Roger Koppl (1991, 204).
9. At the time the federal government had accumulated a debt of $1 trillion, it could borrow an additional $1 billion while inflating at the rate of 10% and not increase its real indebtedness at all. That is, the 10% erosion of the real value of outstanding debt would just offset the current, conventionally defined deficit. The real debt remains constant, and thus the real deficit is taken to be zero. This nominal-to-real adjustment, along with several other such adjustments, underlies Robert Eisner's answer to the question *How Real Is the Federal Deficit?* (1986). Also, see Eisner (1989).
10. The possibility that the effects of deposit-insurance mispricing and the effects of budget-induced uncertainties are intertwined was suggested to me by Jim Barth.

References

Barro, Robert J. "Are Government Bonds Net Wealth?" *Journal of Political Economy* 82 (November-December 1974): 1095–1117.

———. "The Ricardian Approach to Budget Deficits." *Journal of Economic Perspectives* 3, no. 2 (Spring 1989): 37–54.

Barth, James, George Iden, Frank S. Russek, and Mark Wohar. "The Effects of Federal Budget Deficits on Interest Rates and the Composition of Domestic Output." in Rudolph G. Penner, ed., *The Great Fiscal Experiment*. Washington, DC: Urban Institute Press, 1991, 71–141.

Bowles, David, Holly Ulbrich, and Myles Wallace. "Default Risk, Interest Differentials, and Fiscal Policy: A New Look at Crowding Out." *Eastern Economic Journal* 15, no. 3 (July-September 1989): 203–12.

Dewald, William G., and Michael Ulan. "The Twin Deficit Illusion." *Cato Journal* 9, no. 3 (Winter 1989): 689–707.

Dwyer, Gerald P., Jr. "Inflation and Government Deficits." *Economic Inquiry* 20, no. 3 (July 1982): 315–29.

Eisner, Robert. *How Real Is the Federal Deficit?* New York: Free Press, 1986.

———. "Budget Deficits: Rhetoric and Reality." *Journal of Economic Perspectives* 3, no. 2 (Spring 1989): 72–93.

———. "Deficits and Us and Our Grandchildren." in James M. Rock, ed., *Debt and the Twin Deficits Debate*. Mountain View, CA: Mayfield, 1991, 81–107.

Evans, Paul. "Do Large Deficits Produce High Interest Rates?" *American Economic Review* 75, no. 1 (March 1985): 68–87.

Fackler, James S., and W. Douglas McMillin. "Federal Debt and Macroeconomic Activity." *Southern Economic Journal* 55, no. 4 (April 1989): 994–1003.

Garrison, Roger W., Eugenie D. Short, and Gerald P. O'Driscoll, Jr. "Financial Stability and FDIC Insurance." In Catherine England and Thomas Huertas, eds., *The Financial Services Revolution*. Boston: Kluwer 1988, 187–207.

Keynes, John M. *The General Theory of Employment, Interest, and Money*. New York: Harcourt, Brace and World, 1964[1936].

Koppl, Roger. "Animal Spirits." *Journal of Economic Perspectives* 4, no. 3 (Summer 1991): 203–10.

Kormendi, Roger C. "Government Debt, Government Spending, and Private Sector Behavior." *American Economic Review* 73, no. 5 (December 1983): 994–1010.

Machlup, Fritz. "Why Bother about Methodology?" In Machlup, *Methodology in Economics and Other Social Sciences*. New York: Academic, 1978 [1936], 63–70.

Niskanen, William A. "The Uneasy Relation between the Budget Deficit and the Trade Deficit." *Cato Journal* 8, no. 2 (Fall 1988): 507–19.

O'Driscoll, Gerald P., Jr. "The Ricardian Nonequivalence Theorem." *Journal of Political Economy* 85 (February 1977): 207–210.

Roberts, Paul Craig. "Why the Deficit Hysteria is Unjustified." In Richard H.

Fink and Jack C. High, eds., *A Nation in Debt*. Frederick, MD: University Publications of America, 1987, 83–86.

Schultze, Charles L. "Of Wolves, Termites and Pussycats." *Brookings Review* (Summer 1989): 26–33.

Shackle, G. L. S. *Keynesian Kaleidics*. Edinburgh: Edinburgh University Press, 1974.

3

An Empirical Analysis of Public Choice Aspects of the Savings and Loan Disaster

Thomas Havrilesky

Introduction

About the only thing that has grown faster than the tab for the savings and loan mess is the amount of literature devoted to it. Unfortunately, as this literature has snowballed, the proportion of statistical analysis has shrunk. Perhaps the most noticeable shortfall lies in the interstices between the economic and political aspects of the problem. This deficiency persists despite growing interest in politico-economic/public choice theories of banking regulation. Economists are increasingly aware that their earlier emphasis on the market failure theory of regulation caused them to regard too lightly the self-serving behavior of politicians and interest groups that created the present tangle of regulations, subsidies, and taxes and contributed so mightily to the debacle.[1]

The Keating Five fiasco changed all that. Nowadays economists view the savings and loan mess as more than a problem in moral hazard and the economics of bureaucracy. Moreover, they have not been misled by the political witch hunts and scapegoating (e.g., Pizzo, Fricker, and Muolo, 1989; and Adams 1989) that have followed in the wake of the crisis. They recognize that reciprocity between key congresspersons on the one hand and Savings and Loan Political Action Committees (S&L PACs) on the other hand perpetuated the regulatory forbearance that was essential to the subsequent financial holocaust.[2] Modeling reciprocity arrangements is the stock in trade of economists. However, as indicated at the outset, there is a shortage of empirical work here.

The chief purpose of this chapter is to provide empirical grist for public choice analysis. It does so by explaining the campaign contributions of S&L PACs as dependent upon the regulatory philosophies, financial services constituencies, political clout, campaign financing needs, and voting behavior of congresspersons on the Senate and House Banking Committees.

The time span selected is the critical period 1985–1987. There are four reasons for this choice. First, the problem was properly addressed by politicians only after the 1988 elections. Second, over the 1985–1987 interval, S&L PAC-inspired and congressionally directed regulatory forbearance transformed the problem from a $10 billion nuisance into a $150 billion disaster. Third, in these years, key roll call votes and heavy S&L PAC campaign contributions help researchers to identify the influence-peddling guys-with-the-black-hats. Fourth, after mid-1987 S&L PACs realized that the bailout's tab had exceeded their industry's capacity to finance it. With poorly informed taxpayers now footing the bill, solvent S&Ls no longer had to pressure for regulatory forbearance. Their congressional friends could then quietly switch to sombreros of a decidedly lighter hue.

Another feature of this chapter is to explain, over the same time span and with a similar set of variables, the campaign contributions of big bank PACs. This permits an interesting juxtaposition with S&L PAC behavior. Big banks were less threatened by the FSLIC fiasco, except as a probable harbinger of future FDIC problems. Therefore, their PAC's financial largesse might more likely be motivated by a congressperson's regulatory philosophy than by measures of a legislator's political clout. In short, during this critical period the big bank PACs did not try to be as narrowly self-serving as the S&L PACs.

In closing, this chapter draws parallels between the FSLIC catastrophe of the 1980s and the FDIC crisis of the 1990s. Judging from the behavior of the actors in both tragedies, very little has been learned from the empirical lessons outlined in this chapter. Given a rise in interest rates in 1993-94, the FDIC crisis promises to be a replay of its FSLIC harbinger.

The Lack of Leadership

Before we proceed to the empirical analysis, it will be useful to set the institutional stage. This exercise will simultaneously shed light on the origins of the mess and help to explain the lack of forward-looking congressional and administration leadership that allowed the problem to mushroom.

It can scarcely be claimed that politicians were not informed. For example, in 1984 George Bush headed the Committee on Financial Deregulation. Despite the ominous silence on the subject during the 1984 and 1988 presidential election campaigns, the mounting deposit insurance crisis was not exactly a closely guarded secret. Respected economists had been warning about it in widely read publications for years.[3]

Unfortunately, economists' early admonitions were not heeded. There is a painfully simple explanation for this. Politically, economists function primarily as bearers of welcomed falsehoods. Aside from generating forecasts of economic outcomes that are favorable to their politician mentors, economic advisors and their research networks in academia devote most of their energy to legitimating the redistributive programs of their mentors. This type of advocacy is frequently accomplished by cloaking redistributive programs in macroeconomic externalities. As examples, the Keynesian multiplier concept was repeatedly invoked to help legitimate the New Frontier-Great Society redistributive policies of the 1960s, and the precepts of nineteenth-century classical economics were repackaged, labeled "supply side", and invoked to help legitimate the status quo ante tax 1970 cut redistributions of the early 1980s. Despite the obvious ballyhoo, this political smokescreening is apparently taken so seriously by ingenuous academics that it survives to contaminate their research agendas as well as their textbooks. Given their largely ceremonial political roles, economists who foresaw the deposit insurance crisis in the 1970s, having no interest group to propagate their warnings, were voices in the political wilderness.

Why did political leadership fail to avert the disaster? In order for the financial holocaust not to have happened, three centerpieces of modern politics would have to have been, at least partially, dismantled. The first was the philosophy of systematic redistribution in favor of middle-class homeowners, and thereby in favor of the residential construction and financing industries. Since the baby boom of the 1950s, housing had become something of a political sacred cow. Until the mid-1980s, housing tax shelters were a prominent feature of the internal revenue codes. These subsidies came to be viewed as entitlements. Such a formidable cadre of interest groups were appropriating the economic rents associated with these subsidies that it became politically costly for politicians to question them. The second centerpiece, one that had been on politicians' altars for a somewhat shorter period, was financial deregulation. In the mid-1970s financial deregulation rather suddenly became political chic among Republicans and Democrats alike. Facing competition from less regulated sectors and perceiving diminishing net benefits from regulatory barriers and subsidies, powerful industry interest groups prodded politicians onto the financial deregulation bandwagon. For the next decade the financial services sector was fed megadoses of deregulatory elixir without parallel deregulation of deposit insurance. With one hand the politicians encouraged imprudent risk taking by not reforming deposit insurance while with the other hand they removed regulatory barriers to risk taking. As a result, in the 1980s the number of FDIC enforcement actions and bank failures skyrocketed. The third centerpiece had a distinctively Republican burnish: the obsession with low-income tax rates. Long after this idea had outlived its usefulness, its compulsive hold on the administration became something of a political cliché. The reason is that certain interest groups exhibit singleminded devotion to low-income tax rates while other groups have learned to live with the resulting deficit and the high real interest rates that it has entailed.[4]

As executive and legislative leadership clutched these three icons, the greatest financial tragedy in half a century unfolded. Politicians failed to repudiate these three ideas-whose-time-had-gone because they are consummate slow learners. Their learning impediment is totally structural. The polity utilizes information mechanisms that rely upon infrequent, complexly dimensioned signals (voting outcomes, polls, demonstrations, and the results of executive, legislative, and judicial inquiries). Corrective responses to these signals must be filtered through semipermeable regulatory bureaucracies and deeply entrenched political interest groups. Thus, one should not be surprised that politicians consistently fail to recognize and respond to small shifts in the political balance of power, for example, marginal changes in the distribution of voting power within the distribution of earned income, that ideally should prompt them swiftly to reposition themselves on key issues and thereby avoid losses of political support.

Instead of making marginal adjustments to subtle changes in the political environment, politicians tend to cling to shopworn shibboleths, even as they approach the cusp of electoral disaster. How else can one explain Jimmy Carter's blind obeisance to inflationary low interest rates and bracket creep financing, even as bellweather Californians launched taxpayer revolts, senior citizen creditors (who enjoy high interest rates) gathered political strength, and Republican promises of status quo ante tax cuts and anti-inflationary militance were like a huge moving van in front of the White House? How else can one explain Reagan-Bush compulsiveness over low tax rates and deregulation, even as the failure to reregulate deposit insurance, to provide for increased budget appropriations for beleaguered regulators, and to reduce the deficit and real interest rates by raising taxes were creating the biggest financial catastrophe since the Great Depression?

Some Unpleasant Accounting

A prominent theme of the public choice literature is that outright redistributions of after-tax income would be politically disastrous. In an open society institutional camouflage is a necessary but costly complement to all redistributive programs. For this reason, at the time that any particular redistributive program is initiated, the beneficiaries are easily identified, but the losers are markedly more remote and diffuse. During the postwar period of the great politically directed transfer of resources to homeowners, to the residential development, construction, and financing industries, to big, de facto insured depositors as well as to the politicians, regulatory bureaucrats, central bankers, and lobbying groups with whom these beneficiaries had to share the rents,[5] it was difficult to pinpoint the ultimate losers. Now, however, a final accounting is painfully feasible. The first class of losers turned out to be, in the late 1980s, equity holders in depository institutions. The second group of losers is the current generation of homeowners who are suffering sizable losses as a result of massive real estate liquidations by depository institutions and their governmental indemnifiers. The final set of losers will be taxpayers in general, who will, in the 1990s and beyond, be forced to ante up in order to restore the deposit insurance funds (to pay for insured deposits in excess of asset values).

Individual groups of losers aside, great overall social losses befall the nation as a whole. They have arisen and will continue to arise from the massive waste of physical and human capital associated with housing subsidies.

Consider first the misallocation of physical capital. For several decades our nation overinvested in residential development. This resulted in an inadequate replacement of the stock of private as well as public capital goods. A mass of housing was constructed in the 1950s, 1960s, and 1970s at the expense of our industrial base and public infrastructure. Instead of technologically up-to-date capital goods in American industry and an adequate stock of social overhead capital, we have superfluous residential square footage and semivacant shopping centers. Instead of internationally competitive industries, we have underutilized vacation homes to blight our seashores, lakesides, and mountain vistas and redundant commerical strips to disfigure suburban areas.

Of equal importance is the misallocation of human capital. In order to sustain programs for continual subsidization of residential development, lobbying activities had to be supported. In addition, a sizable portion of government expenditures was channeled into the administration of housing-oriented programs. Furthermore, considerable human resources were absorbed by private and public financial institutions that specialized in housing. Also, since the housing lobby was extremely sensitive to interest rates, a considerable share of central bank human resources was allocated to monitoring and manipulating interest rates. Finally, a formidable portion of the human resources of financial institutions was channeled to deciphering the policy moves of the central bank (the Fed-watching industry) (see note 5). Without a properly allocated base of private and public, physical and human capital, our growth rate, real wages, and trade deficit have suffered and will continue to suffer.

The Crisis Mounts: 1980–1985

The Depository Institutions Deregulation and Monetary Control Act of 1980 (DIDMCA) unfettered thrift institutions from their historical dependence on fixed rate mortgages. At the same time Congress, responding to the desires of the S&L lobby, raised the FSLIC deposit insurance ceiling from $40,000 to $100,000, opposed adjustable rate mortgages for thrifts, and lowered S&L net worth requirements from 5% to 3% of assets. The tax cuts of the ensuing year kept interest rates high, and, as a consequence, the profitability of depository institutions suffered. Losses were compounded when S&Ls used their new-found investment powers imprudently. In 1981, 85% of all S&Ls had negative earnings.

In 1981 the regulatory response to the nascent problem was to merge or liquidate only the most crippled institutions, leaving many insolvent thrifts open. Encouraged by the S&L lobby, in 1982 Congress exacerbated the relaxation of regulatory standards by formally codifying it in the Garn-St. Germain Act. Suggestions that regulators might tighten standards were battered down by Congress at the S&L lobby's behest. Accounting sleight-of-hand, such as carrying assets at book rather than market value and counting borrowing from the FHLBB as net worth, was favored by the lobby, endorsed by Congress, and quietly accepted by regulators whose career benefits outweighed the benefits of faithful service. Politicians lost sight of the original purpose of deposit insurance and the principal that public monies should not subsidize private risk taking.

These facts are eloquent testimony to the power and homogeneity of the S&L lobby during this crucial period. They reveal the extent of regulatory capture (Romer and Weingast 1991). They also show that politician principals kept their regulatory agents on short leashes (McCubbins, Noll, and Weingast (1989).

Hopes that a crisis might be diverted began dissolving in 1985 and 1986. The persistent federal budget deficit kept interest rates high. The 1986 tax code revision virtually eliminated real estate shelters. Together with falling oil prices and falling farm prices, these factors depressed real estate values and increased S&L losses in many parts of the country. The crisis began to come to a head in the mid-1980s when Edwin Gray, head of the FHLBB, indicated that $15 billion would be needed to replenish the FSLIC's insurance fund. S&L PACs as a group were not split by the proderegulation/antideregulation breakdown that separated big bank PACs from small bank and nonbank PACs. Troubled S&Ls wanted increased forbearance and limited recapitalization of the fund. Healthy S&Ls, who did not want to pay for a large recapitalization, agreed. Depositors from states with a large percentage of troubled thrifts might have potentially desired a larger recapitalization, but, in 1986, they were badly informed about the potential losses awaiting them. As a result, in 1985–1986 there was hardly any opposition to S&L PACs' demands. Congress supported neither a get-tough regulatory posture nor massive recapitalization. To the contrary, the legislative branch encouraged regulatory laxity by delaying recapitalization of the FSLIC kitty. Poorly policed deregulation and forbearance were career serving for regulatory bureaucrats. As mentioned in the previous section, because of its obsession with deregulation and tolerance of tax-cut-induced budget problems, the administration provided no leadership.

As panicky S&Ls and the insolvency of the FSLIC drove deposit rates up and loan rates down, the profitability of healthy S&Ls suffered and the ranks of the insolvent grew.[6] As a result, within two years the S&L "crisis" had been transformed into an S&L "mess."

The year 1987 was critical. There was mounting concern regarding the cost of recapitalizing the insurance fund. Congresspersons from regions with a high proportion of troubled thrifts were increasingly torn between the desires of the still-powerful and homogeneous S&L PACs for modest recapitalization and forbearance on the one hand and the emerging anxiety of depositors and potential concerns of taxpayers on the other hand. Since forbearance meant that the number of de facto insolvent S&Ls would not significantly decrease and that the size of the subsidy would, perforce, increase, the intensity of S&L PAC pressure on politicians could only grow. At the same time, however, politicians knew that depositors would soon demand massive recapitalization and an end to forbearance. As depositors' concerns mounted, the situation for many legislators reached an inflexion point beyond which they could no longer be counted upon to support the S&L PACs.

Two events mark this political inflexion point.[7] These were the Keating Five scandal and a related, less prominent but equally momentous roll call vote in Congress. The Keating Five affair in April 1987 involved Senators Cranston, De Concini, Glenn, McCain, and Riegle. They met with Charles Keating of Lincoln Savings and Loan and subsequently pressured regulators to give Lincoln a break. Earlier, House Speaker James Wright and Majority Whip Tony Coelho had similarly enjoined regulators on behalf of other savings institutions. The scandal(s) precipitated the roll call vote that also occurred in April 1987. It was on the St. Germain Amendment to HR27 (as discussed below, S790 was the relevant bill in the Senate). The amendment sought to raise FSLIC recapitalization to $15 billion. It was strongly opposed by S&L PACs but openly favored by Speaker Wright and other erstwhile friends of the S&Ls who had been recently tainted by the scandal(s). This vote provides a unique opportunity to examine directly the effect of congressional voting behavior on PAC receipts while controlling for less extraordinary influences such as regulatory philosophies, constituencies, political clout, and campaign needs.

The Causes of Financial PAC Campaign Contributions

In recent years controversy over the power of PACs has intensified. A key political issue is their effect in deterring political competition, as the lion's share (90% of House contributions in 1990) goes to incumbents. Of traditional concern is the issue of whether PAC contributions are rewards for favors received (or expected) by interest groups or merely investments in access to a congressperson. Regardless of which hypothesis is true (and the distinction may be a fuzzy one)[8] public choice analysts want to know what factors condition PAC contributions.[9] In other words, what variables lower the supply price of a congressperson's services to an interest group (Grier and Munger 1991). As long as demand is elastic (as it will normally be), the lower the supply price of a legislator's favors to an interest group, the greater the level of campaign contributions of that group. "Favors" are conceived as units of influence on regulators and legislation. There are five general classes of variables that are prominently mentioned in the literature as influencing this relative supply price: a legislator's regulatory philosophy, constituency, clout, campaign needs, and voting behavior (Poole and Romer 1985; Poole, Romer, and Rosenthal 1987). In what follows I discuss each of these categories.

Regulatory Philosophy

In most cases PACs represent an industry that is affected by at least one regulatory body. In the financial services sector, the overarching regulatory issue of the past two decades has been financial deregulation. After the "level playing field" compromises of the late 1970s, culminating in the Depository Institutions Deregulation and Monetary Control Act of 1980, financial services PACs staked out fairly clear positions on further deregulation. Big bank and S&L PACs remained strong advocates of (more) deregulation. Big bank PACs favored deregulation because it legitimated entry into less regulated markets and a (structural arbitrage) escape route from assessments on their banking assets to replenish the insurance funds. S&L PACs favored deregulation because it promised more profit for their ailing industry. In contrast, nonbank PACs, many of whom were already doing a de facto banking business and whose turf was threatened by the incursion of depository institutions, tended to be a good deal more hesitant regarding further across-the-board deregulation. It threatened to increase the scope of their head-to-head competition with depository institutions. Since conservative congresspersons traditionally have the most favorable attitude toward deregulation, one would expect that legislators with conservative ratings on business issues would have a lower relative supply price of deregulatory influence and would attract relatively more campaign funds from big bank and S&L PACS than from nonbank, small bank, and other financial services PACs.

Constituencies

The regulatory philosophy of a congressperson notwithstanding, the supply price of peddling regulatory influence depends on the preferences of constituents within his or her district or state. The more that constituents are opposed to a position favored by a PAC, the more expensive will be that congressperson's influence, because the greater the cost to him or her in terms of votes and other contributions foregone. In contrast, legislators with sympathetic home constituencies can provide their services more cheaply. In the financial services sector, the greater the economic importance of a particular type of financial institution in a congressperson's home state or district, the lower his or her relative supply price to and the greater the relative contribution of that particular class of PAC.

Clout

Congresspersons who are on committees that deal with the interests of a certain class of PAC have more power to help them than those who are not. This is because committees have the right to hold hearings, to recommend regulatory budgets, and to control the content, timing, and voting on relevant legislation. Within committees, one would expect the more senior members to have greater power, that is, to be able to influence legislation and regulators at lesser cost. Therefore, a legislator's seniority on a committee should affect the *size* of relevant PAC contributions. However, seniority might not affect the relevant PAC *share* of total PAC contributions. For example, if all financial services PACs reward seniority proportionately, then it may be a scalar that would not affect any class of financial PAC's share of total financial PAC contributions. Nevertheless, since the 1985–1987 period was so critical to S&Ls relative to other financial services industries, an increase in a legislator's committee seniority is expected to increase the S&L PACs' share of his or her total financial services PAC campaign contributions.

Campaign Financing Needs

Legislators in close races are generally in greater need of contributions. They would, ceteris paribus, generally be more willing to lower their supply prices to potential contributors. As with clout, however, a measure of a congressperson's needs may be a scalar and not affect the relative contributions of any particular class of PAC.

Voting Behavior

Even if regulatory philosophy, constituencies, and clout dispose a legislator toward being favored by a certain type of PAC, countervailing influences have to be considered. These might include the presence of opposing interests in the legislator's home state or district. For example, if S&Ls are an important component of the financial services sector of a congressperson's district, the existence of anxious depositors during the insurance crisis in 1985–1987 could have counterbalanced S&L PAC influence on that legislator's behavior. Since all such countervailing interests cannot be easily measured, perhaps the best indicator of the relative cost to a PAC of a congressperson's availability to influence regulators is his or her actual voting behavior on issues to which that class of PAC is sensitive.

Empirical Specification

In two separate OLS regressions the dependent variables were the dollar magnitude of the campaign contributions of big bank and thrift PACs respectively during the 1985–1987 period. (A regression for nonbank financial services PACs is reported in Appendix B.) The data set included contributions to each of sixty-eight congresspersons on the House and Senate banking committees expressed as a percentage of total campaign contributions from all financial services PACs.

PAC contributions were obtained from the Federal Elections Commission and required considerable effort to classify. Big bank PACs were defined as organizations that represent commercial banks with assets over $10 billion. Aside from their dominance of total financial services PAC contributions and their obvious impact when joining forces, one reason for the focus on big banks and S&Ls was that specific industry and firm-size orientations of other financial services PACs were more difficult to identify. Another reason was that proposed regulatory legislation in this period specifically affected big commercial banks and S&Ls more than other groups.[10]

There were two regulatory philosophy variables. One was a political party binary measure, assigning a value of one to all Democrats and a value of zero to all Republicans. The other was a legislator's Chamber of Commerce (COC) rating.[11] It was assumed that big banks and S&Ls would be more interested in deregulation, i.e., lowering geographic and product line barriers to entry into financial services markets, than other financial services groups.[12] It was further assumed that deregulation tends to be more favored philosophically by Republicans and by legislators with higer COC ratings. Therefore, the percentage of campaign contributions coming from big bank and S&L PACs was expected to vary directly with these two regulatory philosophy variables.

Constituencies were considered crucial because congresspersons from areas where big banks or S&Ls were relatively unimportant were not expected to receive sizable shares of their financial services PAC campaign contributions from big bank or S&L PACs respectively. Whether a congressperson has large commercial banks in his or her jurisdiction is heavily influenced by the bank branching laws of his or her state. As a measure of the presence of a big bank constituency, we employed a binary variable, assigning a value of one to congresspersons from states with statewide branching and a value of zero to congresspersons from states with limited branching or unit banking. As a measure of an S&L constituency, we used S&L deposits as a ratio of total deposits in the congressperson's state. It was expected that the percentages of big bank and S&L PAC contributions to total financial services PAC contributions would vary directly with these respective variables.

Political clout was measured by the seniority ranking of the legislator on the House or Senate Banking Committee. Because S&Ls

needed political clout more than other financial services industries during the 1985–1987 period, it was expected that the percentage of S&L PAC contributions to total financial services PAC contributions would vary directly with seniority. Because big banks were not in similar straits, it was not expected that the big bank PAC share would be affected by seniority.

Campaign financing needs were measured by the congressperson's plurality in the latest election. It was not expected that S&L PAC or big bank PAC shares would be affected by this measure.

While voting behavior has been linked to campaign contributions from a number of industries in the previous literature—for example, Chappell (1981), Silberman and Durden (1976), and Edelman (1988) —it has never before been done for the financial services sector.[13] Over the entire 1985 to 1987 period there was only one roll call vote taken in either the House or Senate that could clearly be considered either favorable or unfavorable to large banks; this was a 1985 bill to ban credit card surcharges. (Large commercial banks receive significant fee revenues from these charges.) Unfortunately, this measure did not perform well in the empirical tests that follow. Therefore, in its place was used a measure of bill sponsorship. Congresspersons who sponsored legislation that was clearly favorable to big banks were assigned a value of one; all others were assigned a value of zero. (The relevant legislation is described in Appendix A.) It was expected that the percentage of total financial services PAC contributions received from big bank PACs would vary positively with this measure.

With regard to S&Ls the key roll call vote was on the St. Germain Amendment to HR27 in the House and a related amendment to S790 in the Senate. The House amendment proposed raising FSLIC recapitalization from $5 billion to $15 billion. The U.S. Savings and Loan League opposed the amendment. The Senate amendment proposed raising FSLIC capitalization to only $7.5 billion. It was favored by the league. These relatively close votes (the House vote was 153–258) indicate divided ranks on the recapitalization issue. As discussed earlier, many legislators were becoming sensitive to depositor concerns associated with adverse publicity arising from pressuring regulators for forbearance. Those voting against the House amendment or for the Senate amendment were assigned a value of one; those voting for the House amendment, against the Senate amendment, or not voting were assigned a value of zero. It was expected that the percentage of total financial services PAC contri-

Table 3.1
Dependent Variable: Big Bank PAC Contributions as a Percentage of Total Financial Services PAC Contributions, 1985–1987 (t statistics in parentheses)

Intercept	*Party*	*Chamber of Commerce Rating*	
-0.1506	0.0396	0.0025**	
(-1.524)	(0.841)	(2.965)	
State Branching Status	*Voting Record*	*Seniority*	*Plurality*
0.0574**	0.1236**	0.00456*	0.1374
(2.040)	(2.495)	(1.957)	(1.455)

No. of observations = 52
R^2 = .30

** Significant at the .05 level
* Significant at the .10 level

butions received from S&L PACs would vary directly with this binary measure.

As mentioned earlier there is a problem of multicollinearity when voting behavior and variables that are highly correlated with voting behavior are included as explanatory variables in the same regression. In addition, there is a reverse causality problem associated with measuring legislator's voting behavior and their PAC receipts in the same period. Rational legislators might anticipate their PAC contributions and vote accordingly, thus causing confusion of cause and effect. One way to reduce these problems is to choose votes that came as authentic behaviorial suprises to the PACs.[14] To some extent HR27 fits this description since many of their erstwhile friends abandoned the S&L PACs on this vote. Another way to reduce both problems is to drop all voting variables as explanatory variables in the regression. In the following section the results will be discussed with and without the voting behavior variables.

Results

Table 3.1 reports the OLS results for big bank PAC contributions. Of the two regulatory philosophy variables, only the Chamber of Commerce (COC) rating was statistically significant and had the expected sign. The estimate indicates that voting on the probusiness side just 10% more of the time will increase a congressperson's big bank PAC share of total financial services PAC contributions by 2%.[15] In contrast, the estimated coefficient for the political party binary variable was not statistically significant at a high level of significance.[16]

The estimated coefficient for the bank size constituency variable was also statistically significant and had the expected sign. Congresspersons from statewide branching states received over 5.7% more campaign contributions from big bank PACs as a share of total financial services PAC contributions than their counterparts in limited branching or unit banking states.

The estimated coefficient for the bill sponsorship binary variable was statistically significant and had the expected sign. Sponsorship or cosponsorship of a pro-big bank bill increased a congressperson's big bank PAC share of total financial services PAC contributions by 12%.

The estimated coefficient for the seniority variable was also statistically significant. A one-step increase in a legislator's seniority ranking, a unit reduction in the explanatory variable, decreased the dependent variable by approximately .4%.[17] This result was somewhat of a surprise. Because of the adding-up constraint, it likely reflects the effects, reported below, that an increase in seniority has in increasing a congressperson's S&L and nonbank PAC shares of total financial services PAC contributions.[18]

As expected, the estimated coefficient for the plurality variable was not statistically significant.

When the bill sponsorship binary is dropped because of potential multicollinearity and reverse causality, the sign and statistical significance of the estimated coefficients do not change. When the political party binary is dropped, there is a similar absence of changes.

Table 3.2 reports the OLS results for S&L PAC contributions.[19] For the two regulatory philosophy variables the estimated coefficients were statistically significant only at the .13 level of significance. Moreover, the sign of the coefficient for the political party variable surprisingly was positive (see note 12). Because they were focusing their attention on the crucial bread-and-butter issue of recapitalization and forbearance during this period, S&L PACs may not have cared about legislators' regulatory philosophy.

The estimated coefficient for the S&L constituency variable was statistically significant and had the expected sign. As S&L deposits as a percentage of total deposits rose by 10%, a congressperson's

Table 3.2
Dependent Variable: S&L PAC Contributions as a Percentage of Total Financial Services PAC Contributions, 1985–1987 (t statistic in parentheses)

Intercept	*Party*	*Chamber of Commerce Rating*
0.0258	0.0682	0.0011
(-0.266)	(1.514)	(1.552)

State S&L Deposits as a Percentage of Total Deposits	*Voting Record*	*Seniority*	*Plurality*
0.2372*	0.0574*	-0.0035*	-0.0656
(1.860)	(1.947)	(-1.718)	(-0.077)

R^2 = .29
No. of observations = 52

* Significant at .10 level

S&L PAC share of total financial services PAC contributions rose by 2.4%. Apparently, in the 1985–87 period, depositors and taxpayers were not yet sufficiently informed and organized to cause legislators from states where S&Ls were important to ignore their PAC's pressures for continued forbearance and low recapitalization.

The estimated coefficient for the voting record variable was also statistically significant and had the expected sign. A House vote against raising recapitalization from $5 billion to $15 billion or a Senate vote for raising recapitalization to $7.5 billion generated a 5.7% increase in a legislator's S&L PAC share of total financial services PAC contributions.[20]

The seniority variable was statistically significant and had the expected sign. If a legislator moved up one step in seniority on the Banking Committee, a unit reduction in the explanatory variable, it generated a .3.5% rise in the contributions that he or she received from S&L PACs expressed as a share of total financial services PAC contributions. This result supports the conjecture that during the critical 1985–1987 period S&L PACs had a greater need for political clout than other financial services PAC.

Finally, similar to the case of big bank PAC contributions in Table 3.1, the plurality variable was again statistically insignificant.

When the vote binary is dropped because of potential

multicollinearity and reverse causality, the sign and significance of the estimated coefficients do not change except that the estimate for the party binary becomes statistically significant at the .05 level. When the party binary is dropped, the estimate for the Chamber of Commerce rating variable loses statistical significance and the estimates for the S&L constituency and seniority variables are only significant at the .13 level.

Concluding Comment

Public choice theory suggests that politicians are motivated by rent seeking. In particular, the campaign contributions of political action committees are an important benefit that politicians can presumably garner by adopting attitudes toward regulation that are favorable to certain classes of PACs.

The present article focuses on S&L and big bank PACs because they have never before been studied in this context, their campaign contributions are formidable, they are fairly easily identified, and there is controversial legislation on which they have taken a strong stand and for which roll call votes are available. It develops statistical evidence regarding the factors that affect big bank and S&L PAC campaign contributions, thereby adding to what is known about the S&L disaster.

During the 1985–1987 period the campaign contributions of big bank and S&L PACs, each expressed as a share of total financial services PAC contributions, appear to have been similarly motivated by measures of voting behavior. If a legislator sponsored or cosponsored a pro-big bank bill, his or her proportionate big bank PAC contributions rose, and if he or she voted for a pro-S&L bill, his or her proportionate S&L PAC contributions rose.

Moreover, big bank PAC and S&L PAC contributions, expressed as shares of total financial services PAC contributions, were also similarly affected by measures of the importance of big bank and S&L constituencies in legislators' home states. Congresspersons from statewide branching states received a significantly greater proportion of their campaign contributions from big bank PACs. In addition, an increase in S&L deposits as a percentage of total deposits in a congressperson's state increased his or her proportionate share of contributions from S&L PACs.

Regulatory philosophy, as measured by a legislator's Chamber of Commerce rating, had an effect on proportionate big bank PAC contributions but not on proportionate S&L PAC contributions. The more conservative the legislator's Chamber of Commerce rating, the larger the big bank PAC contribution as a share of total financial services PAC contributions. Regulatory philosophy as measured by political party affiliation did not have a statistically significant effect on either class of PAC contributions.

Another difference between the two classes of PAC contributions is associated with the effect of political clout as measured by committee seniority. This variable had a significant, positive effect on S&L PAC contributions, presumably because S&Ls were more in need of political clout during the critical 1985–1987 period.

Finally, both dependent variables were not significantly affected by campaign financing needs, as measured by plurality in the previous election.

Implications for the FDIC Crisis: The More Things Change . . .

In view of the painful lessons learned from the S&L disaster, the ingenuous onlooker would probably not expect an instant replay in the banking industry. Unfortunately, in comparing the FDIC crisis of the 1990s to the FSLIC crisis of the 1980s, one finds that very little has changed.

The FSLIC disaster should have reminded politicians of the traditional principle that public monies should *not* subsidize private risk taking. Instead it seems to have taught them that they *must* subsidize private risk taking.

This chapter shows that the S&L PACs prevented regulators from reining in the risk-taking activities of large institutions before their depleted net worth transformed them into parasites on the insurance fund. Once the fund had dried up, implosive forces took hold that could not be offset by lower interest rates, granting the industry's broader investment powers, or the infusion of taxpayer's monies.

The script for the current FDIC tragedy is almost identical. Big bank PACs support regulatory discretion in the closing of failed institutions and refuse to oppose the too-big-to-fail doctrine. The FDIC has never allowed the uninsured depositors of banks over $1 billion in assets to suffer losses. (Todd and O'Driscoll, this volume). Risk taking by and consolidation among large insolvent institutions steadily increases their dependency on the FDIC (White, this volume). The list of walking wounded money center banks is well known.

The nursing of disabled banks in the early 1990s with lower reserve requirements, aberrantly lower short-term interest rates (through discount window and open market operations), broader geographic and product line powers, and a prospective infusion of taxpayers' monies is proceeding in much the same manner as the nursing of the insolvent thrifts in the 1980s. Unfortunately, just as in the 1980s, many of the patients are not recovering and given a significant rise in interest rates an implosion of the banking industry and a taxpayer bailout of the fund are imminent (Kaufman, this volume).

A tragic irony is that market forces and public policy are diametrically opposed. Market forces would eliminate many of our largest banks while the too-big-to-fail doctrine, by stimulating consolidation among the largest banks and providing uninsured depositors with glowing incentives to shift funds to them, pushes the industry in the opposite direction. Taxpayers' wealth is being used to keep the largest banks alive. Just as in the 1980s, with one hand politicians encourage additional risk taking through de facto deposit insurance coverage, while with the other hand they continue to lower regulatory barriers. This can only mean a costly replay of the S&L holocaust.

The parallel persists because there are no incentives for the actors in the tragedy to perform otherwise. Politicians still cling to the same sacred cows and engage in the same self-deception. Their ties with powerful industry interest groups are, if anything, stronger. Regulators and central bankers are reluctant to oppose wholeheartedly the too-big-to-fail doctrine because it has not been opposed by the PACs. As in the 1980s, taxpayers and small depositors are diffuse, disorganized and ready for their fleecing and the next round of postdisaster scapegoating.

As in the 1980s, there is moverment toward reform: tougher balance sheet standards enacted by high-minded public servants and presumably enforced by untouchable regulators. Unfortunately, the public choice perspective on reform is decidely more pessimistic. Entrenched interest groups continue to impede enforcement at the expense of the industry that regulations were designed to protect. For example, the 1991 bank reform bill did nothing to stop tottering banks from temporarily hiding behind the too-big-to-fail doctrine, masking their insolvency, betting on rescue from permanenly lower short-term interest rates, while systematically overbidding for deposits and gambling on high-risk investments.

Unless we sever the link between expected electoral success and manipulation of regulatory policy, economic well-being will continue to be sacrificed in the name of political expediency. With so many interest groups benefiting from the political rentseeking that permeates regulatory policy, meaningful reform is unlikely. Nevertheless, as recurrent regulatory policy crises indicate, the costs in terms of the erosion of economic health are formidable.

Appendix A

Bill Sponsorship

These were the five bills sponsored in 1987–1988 that were assessed to be clearly favorable to big banks (see note 11).

1. Comprehensive Bank Restructuring, Powers, and Safety Act. Amend banking and securities laws to minimize hazard to federally insured financial institutions from securities, insurance, and real estate activities; develop and test structures for bank holding companies to prevent unfair competition in delivery of certain securities, insurance, real estate services; establish functional regulation of financial institutions by providing that bank security activities be carried on in separate security affiliates of bank holding companies subject to Securities and Exchange Commission (SEC) oversight; establish Financial Intermediaries Review Commission to analyze, report, and make recommendations to Congress regarding future banking institutions' possible combining with financial and commercial firms.

2. Competitive Equality Banking Act. An original bill to regulate nonbank banks, impose a moratorium on certain securities and insurance activities by banks, recapitalize the Federal Savings and Loan Insurance Corporation (FSLIC), allow emergency interstate bank acquisitions, streamline credit union operations, regulate consumer checkholds, and for other purposes.

3. A bill to perserve the authority of the federal banking supervisory agencies to arrange interstate acquisitions and mergers for failed or failing banks, and for other purposes.

4. Dual Banking System Enhancement and Financial Services Competitiveness Act. A bill to enhance the competitiveness of commercial banks and bank holding companies.

5. Banking Reform and Community Benefits Act. A bill to enhance the competitiveness of commercial banks and bank holding

Table 3.3
Dependent Variable: Nonbank PAC Contributions as a Percentage of Total Financial Services PAC Contributions, 1985–1987 (t statistics in parentheses)

Intercept	*Party*	*Chamber of Commerce Rating*	
0.9698	-0.0911	-0.0053*	
(5.893)	(-1.161)	(-3.794)	
State Branching Status	*Voting Record*	*Seniority*	*Plurality*
0.0143	-0.1899*	-0.0160*	-0.1841
(0.305)	(-2.301)	(-4.109)	(-1.171)

No. of observations = 52
$R^2 = .38$

* Significant at the .05 level

companies in the securities market, to ensure that commercial banks and bank holding companies engaged in securities activities will provide their communities with additonal benefits, and for other purposes.

Appendix B

The Campaign Contributions of Nonbank Financial Services PACs

The main purpose of this chapter was to compare the determinants of S&L and big bank PAC contributions to legislators on the House and Senate Banking Committees. When small bank PAC contributions were examined in similar frameworks, the results were mildly disappointing (see note 19). However, the results for the contributions of nonbank financial services PACs as a share of total financial services PAC contributions were quite interesting. Since the interests of big banks and nonbank financial services firms are often at odds in regulatory matters, one would expect the estimated coefficients for the voting record and regulatory philosophy variables in an equation with the contributions of nonbank financial services PAC as the dependent variable to be opposite in algebraic sign.

Table 3.3 reports the OLS results for nonbank financial services

PAC contributions. The estimated coefficient for the bill sponsorship binary was negative and statistically significant. Congresspersons who sponsored or cosponsored pro-big bank legislation received an 18% decrease in their contributions from nonbank PACs as a share of total financial services PAC contributions.

Of the two regulatory philosophy variables, only the Chamber of Commerce rating was statistically significant. Not surprisingly, the sign was negative. The estimate indicates that voting on the probusiness/proderegulation side 10% more of the time will decrease a congressperson's nonbank PAC share of total financial services PAC contributions by over 5%.

The estimated coefficients for the branching status and plurality variables were statistically insignificant. The seniority variable was statistically significant. A one-step increase in committee seniority, a unit decrease in the explanatory variable, generated a 1.6% increase in the nonbank PAC share of total financial services PAC contributions.

When the bill sponsorship binary is dropped because of potential multicollinearity and reverse causality, the sign and significance of the estimated coefficients do not change. When the political party binary is dropped, there is a similar absence of changes.

Notes

Thanks go to John Gildea, James Granato, Edward Kane, and the participants in the New York University Conference on the Crisis in the Banking Industry for helpful suggestions and to Todd Gilmer and Scott Jaquette for computational assistance.

1. A contrast and comparison of market failure and public choice approaches to banking regulation appears in Havrilesky (1989). The market failure view envisions politicians regulating in the public interest, industry circumventing these regulations, and politicians continually reregulating again in the public interest. The public choice view is that regulations at any time reflect the competing self-interested political influences of industry and consumer groups who seek protection from the market whenever it is politically feasible.
2. There are plenty of examples of analysts who, having keenly monitored this problem for many years, now place heavier emphasis on the public choice approach. For instance, Brumbaugh (1988) and Barth and Brumbaugh (1990).

3. As a coeditor of three editions of a book of readings in banking and financial markets and institutions beginning in the mid-1970s, I was aware of the early warnings from respected economists that appeared in widely read publications throughout the early 1970s. See, for example, the articles by Thomas Mayer, Ronald Watson, and Jack Guttentag in Havrilesky and Boorman (1976). The bibliographies of these articles indicate that the literature on this subject goes back at least as far as the 1960s.
4. It can also be argued that the uncertainty regarding which sectors will bear the burden of deficit financing is preferred by politicians to the certainty regarding which will bear the burden of explicit taxation. See Garrison (this volume).
5. The total cost of lobbying for maintaining and camouflaging these redistributions is sizable. It includes not only the expenses of maintaining the residential construction, development, and financing lobbies but also government expenditures for administering programs that benefit housing. Furthermore, since these lobbies were extremely sensitive to interest rates, the total cost of these redistributions also includes a sizable portion of the expenses of our monetary policy institutions. These include the costs of monetary policy misdirection (a big share of the cost of running the Fed), the costs of maintaining a private Fed-watching industry, and the costs of sustaining private and public sector pressures on monetary policy. Finally, since the housing lobbies continually pressured for low interest rates that were usually inflationary, the total cost of these redistributions would also include a good deal of the social cost of inflation.
6. The Supply Side Coup of 1985–1986 and the subsequent shift to easy monetary policy may have been directed not only toward reducing the value of the dollar in order to relieve export-oriented and import-threatened industries but also toward lowering interest rates in order to help the troubled S&Ls.
7. This label suggests more precise identification than actually possible. There was considerable political jostling, shifting, and repositioning even after April of 1987, with some legislators returning to a proforbearance stance.
8. Much of the earlier literature models the rewards versus bribe aspects of campaign contributions, for example, Welch (1974) and Zion and Eytan (1974). This distinction disappears when *expected* rewards and *expected* politician responses are introduced to the model.
9. There is the possibility that PAC contributions are not motivated by political considerations at all but reflect a return for private benefits received from a congressperson's law practice or business firm. Data on banking clients of such firms could not be obtained.
10. Expressing contributions as shares was the result of focusing on osten-

sibly heterogeneous subsectors of the financial services sector and the legislators appurtenant thereto. Big bank PACs contributed $1,076,329 to these congresspersons in 1985–1987. Thrift PACs contributed $878,493. All other financial services PACs combined contributed a total of $4,006,828. The "all other" category included PACs representing smaller banks, PACS representing nonbank financial services industries, PACs representing the customers of financial services firms, and a miscellaneous category.

11. The potential for multicollinearity from having two regulatory philosophy variables in the same regression is discussed below. The Chamber of Commerce rates the percentage that each congressperson voted favorably to the business side on representative pieces of business legislation. Ideally, one would want to employ a similar rating system developed by the banking industry. Such a rating system does not exist.
12. Even though big banks and S&Ls have historically tended to oppose nonbank entry into traditional (commercial loan and checkable deposits) markets, competitiveness in these markets has increased significantly in the past two decades. Consequently, there has been more to gain from big banks promoting their own entry into nonbanking areas such as investment banking rather than from their inhibiting nonbank entry into traditional banking markets. Similarly, S&Ls had more to gain from capturing broader investment powers than from impeding nonbank encroachment into their traditional markets.
13. The use of voting variables as explanatory variables gives rise to problems of multicollinearity and reverse causality in the statistical analysis. These problems are discussed below.
14. For an attempt to deal with the reverse causuality problem in this way, see Havrilesky, "Causes and Consequences" (1990b).
15. In a separate test the Chamber of Commerce rating was entered in various nonlinear transformations in order to capture a conjectured clustering of sizable contributions to congresspersons near the rating median. The premise was that mugwump legislators would be easier to influence on regulatory issues. None of the transformations produced statistically significant estimates.
16. The earlier literature supports the belief that party lines are not important, arguing that since there is low and decreasing turnover of incumbents, PAC access must be maintained (by PAC contributions) regardless of party affiliation. Because of possible multicollinearity with the Chamber of Commerce rating variable, the party variable was dropped from this equation. When this was done there was no effect on the sign or significance of the other estimates and a very small reduction in the R2.
17. A binary variable measuring whether the congressperson was chair of the House or Senate Banking Committee was also tried in both equations but was not statistically significant.

18. A binary variable measuring whether the congressperson was a freshman was also tried in both equations but was not statistically significant.
19. An equation was estimated with the contributions of smaller bank PACs as a share of total financial services PAC contributions as the dependent variable. The explanatory variables were the same as in Table 3.1. Except for the state branching status binary, whose estimated coefficient was negative, and the Chamber of Commerce index, whose estimated coefficient was positive, all estimated coefficients were statistically insignificant.
    The result was:

Table 3.4

Intercept	*Party*	*Chamber of Commerce Rating*
0.0111	0.02503	0.0009*
(0.186)	(0.875)	(1.772)

State Branching Status	*Voting Record*	*Seniority*	*Plurality*
-0.0322*	0.0172	-0.0001	0.0250
(-1.886)	(0.573)	(0.020)	(0.437)
$R^2 = .03$			

* Significant at the .10 level

20. A binary variable measuring whether the congressperson was implicated in the House Speaker Wright or Keating Five scandals was also tried here but was not statistically significant. Only Senators Riegle and Cranston were members of the Keating Five and were also on the Senate Banking Committee.

References

Adams, James Ring. 1989. *The Big Fix: Inside the S&L Scandal.* New York: Wiley, 1989.

Barth, James R., and R. Dan Brumbaugh. "The Rough Road from FIRREA to Deposit Insurance Reform." *Stanford Law & Policy Review* (Spring 1990): 58–67.

Brumbaugh, R. Dan. *Thrifts under Siege: Restoring Order to American Banking.* Cambridge, MA: Ballinger, 1988.

Chappell, Henry W. "Campaign Contributions and Voting on the Cargo Preference Bill: A Comparison of Simultaneous Models." *Public Choice* 36 (1981).

Edelman, Susan A. "Get 'Em While They're Green: Corporate PACs and Congressional Freshmen." Manuscript, April 1988.

Grier, Kevin B., and Michael C. Munger. "Committee Assignments, Constituent Preferences, and Campaign Contributions." *Economic Inquiry* 29 (1991): 24–44.

Havrilesky, Thomas. "The Influence of the Federal Advisory Council on Monetary Policy." *Journal of Money, Credit and Banking* 22 (1990a).

———. "The Causes and Consequences of Big Bank PAC Contributions." *Journal of Financial Services Research* 4 (1990b): 243–249.

———. "Market Failure and Public Choice Theories of Banking Regulation Deregulation." *Research in Financial Services* 1 (1989): 129–50.

Havrilesky, Thomas, and John Boorman (eds.). *Current Perspectives in Banking*. Arlington Heights, 12; Harlan Davidson, 1976.

Kane, Edward J. "The Gathering Crisis in Federal Deposit Insurance." Cambridge: MIT Press, 1985.

———. "The Unending Deposit Insurance Mess." *Science* 27 (1989): 451–56.

McCubbins, Mathew D., Roger G. Noll, and Barry R. Weingast. "Structure and Process, Politics and Policy: Administrative Arrangements and the Political Control of Agencies." *Virginia Law Review* 75 (1989): 431–82.

Pizzo, Stephen P., Mary Fricker, and Paul Muolo. *Inside Job: The Looting of America's Savings and Loans*. New York: McGraw-Hill, 1989.

Poole, Keith, and Thomas Romer. "Patterns of Political Action Committee Contributions to the 1980 Campaign for the United States House of Representatives." *Public Choice* 47 (1985).

Poole, Keith, Thomas Romer, and Howard Rosenthal. "The Revealed Preferences of Political Action Committees." *American Economic Review* (May 1987).

Romer, Thomas, and Barry Weingast. "Political Foundations of the Thrift Debacle." In A. Alesina, ed., *Politics and Economics in the 1980s*. Chicago: University of Chicago Press, 1991.

Silberman, Jonathan, and Garey Durden. "Determining Legislative Preferences on the Minimum Wage: An Economic Approach." *Journal of Political Economy* 84 (1976).

Tullock, Gordon. *The Economics of Rent-Seeking*. Boston: Kluwer, 1989.

Weingast, Barry R. "The Congressional-Bureaucratic System: A Principal-Agent Perspective (with Applications to the SEC)." *Public Choice* 44 (1984): 147–91.

Weingast, Barry R., and Mark J. Moran. "Bureaucratic Discretion or Congressional Control? Regulatory Policymaking by the Federal Trade Commission." *Journal of Political Economy* 91 (1983): 765–800.

Welch, William P. "The Economics of Campaign Funds." *Public Choice* 20 (1974).

Zion, Uri, and Zeev Eytan. "On Money Votes and Policy in a Democratic Society." *Public Choice* 17 (1974).

4

Bankers as Scapegoats for Government-Created Banking Crises in U.S. History

Richard M. Salsman

Introduction

If there is anything more tragic than our current banking crisis, it is that the crisis is being blamed on the wrong group, on the bankers, instead of on the primary culprit, government intervention. The tragedy lies in failing to identify the fundamental cause of the problem, thereby ensuring its continuance. Bankers are not entirely innocent of wrongdoing in the present debacle, but to the extent that bankers have been irresponsible, it has been primarily government intervention that has encouraged them to be so. More widely, it is irresponsible government policy that has made the U.S. banking crises of the past century so frequent and seemingly so inevitable. Government has created these banking crises—sometimes inadvertently, at other times with full knowledge—by making it nearly impossible to practice prudent banking. Having done so, government has then pointed to bad banking practices as sufficient cause for still further interventions in the industry.

I. The Context of the Current Banking Crisis

The view that today's banking crisis is due primarily to the mismanagement and fraud of private bankers underlies most popular accounts of the crisis.[1] Critics are inclined to blame private bankers for banking instability because they wrongly believe that unregulated banking systems are inherently unstable and that regulation is required to restrain some natural tendency of private bankers to engage in mismanagement and fraud. Central banking is said to provide a restraining influence on the destabilizing urges of the private banking system, while free banking is seen as inherently prone to instability. The recent, burgeoning literature on free banking overthrows this conventional wisdom and defends free banking as an inherently stable system made unstable only by legal restrictions and central banking-related interventions.[2] In this view, bad banking comes not from free markets but from perverse public policy.

Guided by erroneous assumptions about the nature of free banking and central banking, analysts of the current crisis typically stress the symptoms (bad banking practices), and overlook the underlying disease (government intervention), as the cause of our problems. For example, many commentators and bank regulators are satisfied to cite anecdotal evidence from the current banking crisis to draw the obvious conclusion that bankers like Charles Keating are incompetent and dishonest, and then to claim that these and similar cases represent the sum and substance of an explanation of the banking crisis. Such figures simply are not representative of the entire industry. While there is no denying that bankers such as Charles Keating exist, we can only understand the fundamental cause of our banking crisis by identifying the institutional arrangements that make such bankers possible. As I argue below, central banking and legal restrictions have institutionalized unsafe banking.

Today's banking crisis is only the latest in a long series of U.S. banking crises blamed on bankers but actually caused by government intervention. A quick review of our banking history makes the point. The mere mention of "wildcat banking" conjures up images of reckless banking practices on the American frontier in the nineteenth century, even though it was government intervention that promoted such practices.[3] "Money panics" in the late nineteenth century were always cause for alarm, political demagoguery, and reform movements aimed at checking the "power" of bankers, even though government intervention brought on those panics as well.[4] The stock market crash of 1929 and the collapse of more than a third of all banks in the Great Depression of the early 1930s were blamed on "excesses" in the financial system and by the bankers of the time, although it was later demonstrated that irresponsible Federal Reserve policy created the boom and the bust.[5] In the past decade, the stupendous demise of the S&L industry, the breakdown of commercial banking, and the collapse of deposit insurance are only the latest examples of crisis in American banking. But these too, are scandals laid primarily at the feet of the bankers, even though government intervention made them possible (Salsman 1990).

In the next section I discuss the nature of banking crises and offer a framework for understanding why bankers are made scapegoats for such crises. In the following sections I discuss three important banking episodes in the United States over the past century, episodes not only characterized by crisis but also followed by reforms intended to preclude future crises: 1) the money panics of the late nineteenth century, especially the panic of 1907, and the Federal Reserve System that followed, 2) the banking collapse of the early 1930s, which brought still further reforms, and 3) the banking problems of the late 1970s that were again followed by reforms in the early 1980s aimed at preventing future instability. Finally, I examine the current banking crisis in light of the historical pattern. In each of these cases I show how misguided reforms flowed naturally from the view that bankers, not government, caused the crises, and that the reforms only perpetuated future instability instead of fundamentally curing it. The historical pattern is as tragic as it is repetitive, because the recurring failure to properly identify government intervention as the culprit in these banking crises has brought only further interventions and further crises. Only if we understand the pattern and break it can we undertake truly effective reform.

II. The Nature of Banking Crises and the Need for Scapegoats

Historically, banking crises have been characterized as either temporary scrambles for liquidity lasting a few weeks or months, or prolonged periods of banking deterioration involving not only illiquidity but also falling asset prices, declining solvency, and bank failure extending over a few years. The "money panics" in the United States during the national banking era are examples of the former type of crisis, while the banking collapse of the early 1930s is an example of the latter type. As Anna J. Schwartz (1986) has observed, the occasional distress suffered by overextended debtors is not sufficient to warrant the label "crisis"; only major disruptions in the payments system or widespread credit defaults closely associated with breakdowns in money itself fit the bill. Moreover, bank runs of limited scope or depositor runs on a limited number of particular banks do not constitute a crisis. Rather, crises entail widespread failures or runs on the banking system itself (Calomiris and Gorton 1991; Tallman 1988).

Where do the fundamental origins of banking crises lie? Some have argued that fractional reserve banking is inherently prone to panics, because deposits that can be withdrawn on demand are primarily invested in longer-term assets instead of cash. But recent research has shown that countries other than the United States with fractional reserve systems have been panic free and that "banking panics are not inherent in banking contracts—institutional structure matters" (Calomiris and Gorton 1991). The phrase "institutional structure" designates the legal and economic framework within which banks operate. Some frameworks clearly promote stability, while others invite crises.

That bankers could be the source of banking crises seems a remote possibility, considering the damage to the health and reputation of the industry that panics bring. There is little evidence in economic theory or history to suggest that private bankers—any more than businesspeople in other fields—would naturally tend to disrupt or destroy their own industry, and therefore their own livelihoods. There is considerable evidence, on the other hand, that governments tend to work to the detriment of the market. The "public choice" revolution in economics has overturned the long-held assumption that government actions are conducted in the "public interest." Instead, the public choice school holds that government pursues its own power, one that is often at odds with optimal market outcomes. Public choice insights about governmental power seeking call for a new perspective on central banking and banking regulation. I have argued elsewhere (Salsman 1990, 119–24) that the primary purpose of central banking is to finance larger government, to provide funds above and beyond those obtained through taxing and borrowing powers. In the United States, such funds have been needed to finance wars, including the Civil War and World War I, but also to finance a growing welfare state that began in the progressive era, when the Federal Reserve was created. Other writers (Goodhart 1988; Glasner 1989, ch. 2) have located the origins of foreign central banks, as well, in governments' desire to secure access to financial resources by endowing particular banks with monopoly powers over money. The basic revenue-raising purpose of central banking carries with it a functional tendency to undermine the financial condition of the private banking system (Salsman 1990, 39–78). The powerful interventions of government central banks and the extensive legal restrictions imposed on the actions of private banks are therefore an obvious starting point for discerning the source of banking instability.

A public choice perspective leads to skepticism about the traditional rationales for central banking and bank regulation. History turns out to warrant such skepticism. The traditional "public interest" perspective claimed that central banks were needed to "fight inflation" or "promote economic growth" or "lower interest rates" or "smooth the business cycle" or "insure full employment." Prior to the establishment of central banking in this century, however, the United States enjoyed much lower inflation and interest rates, greater rates of economic growth, narrower cyclical swings, and lower unemployment. Bank regulation is traditionally justified on the grounds that bankers are reckless in its absence. But extensive research has shown that bankers are more reckless when they have access to government deposit insurance and a lender of last resort, attributes not of free markets but of central banking regimes (Benston et al. 1986).

Public choice theory can also inform us about the tendency of government to make bankers scapegoats for banking crises. Although governments take actions that undermine markets, they do not wish to be seen as disrupters of markets or destroyers of the living standards markets deliver. By deflecting attention away from their own disruptive actions toward those of a scapegoat, governments can escape voter wrath and preserve their powers for another day. If banking crises were widely attributed to central banking and legal restrictions—as they were in Andrew Jackson's day—there might be general agitation for the removal of such interventions. Governments that benefit from central banking and legal restrictions will naturally promote an alternative view.

It is true that government officials in the United States have been blamed in part for today's banking crisis, but seldom in a way that questions government intervention at root. The U.S. government is more often blamed for allegedly "deregulating" banks, for being insufficiently strict in its regulatory oversight, or for being too eager to protect unscrupulous bank executives from regulatory scrutiny. In such cases government is blamed, not for promoting instability through intervention, but for being insufficiently interventionist.

We turn now to an examination of historic banking crises in the

United States, showing how and why bankers have been made scapegoats for government-sponsored instability.

III. Money Panics and Banking Crises in the National Banking Era: Precursor to the Federal Reserve System

During the "national banking era" in the United States (1863–1913), the banking system suffered periodic "money panics" that were significant enough to provoke government investigations—and growing criticism—of private banking practices. Throughout this era, all currency-issuing U.S. banks operated under legal restrictions imposed by the National Currency Acts of 1863 and 1864.[6] Since the investigations generally failed to recognize that the crises were caused by legal restrictions on banks, they paved the way for banking reforms that extended government interventions still further in money and banking.

Historians have identified five episodes of "money panics," or banking crises, in the fifty years between the Civil War and the formation of the Fed in 1913. The banking crises occurred in the years 1873, 1884, 1890, 1893, and 1907.[7] These crises differed considerably from the crises experienced in the twentieth century, the era of central banking. They were briefer, milder, and involved acute illiquidity, whereas in this century crises have involved prolongued periods of recession and depression, widespread bank failure, and chronic insolvency. That the basic solvency of banks was not an issue during the national banking era is confirmed by the relative capital strength of the banking system, even during the five crises. For example, in 1893, the banking system enjoyed a capital ratio (capital as a percent of total assets) of 25%, nearly four times the level maintained by banks today (Salsman 1990, 107).

During the occasional bouts of illiquidity that arose in the post-Civil War banking system, depositors and banks found it difficult, if not impossible, to convert deposits into currency. The illiquidity that did arise was seasonal in nature, not secular; on an absolute level, the liquidity ratio of the banking system (cash assets as a percent of demand deposits) appeared to be high during the national banking era (above 20%), again, well above the ratios maintained by banks today. However, the sharp, seasonal variations in liquidity and occasionally large differences in the relative liquidity levels of particular banks proved troublesome. In some cases banks attempted to build liquidity during crises by contracting call loans, instead of preserving it by suspending the convertibility of deposits. In this respect, depositors were less harmed by the illiquidity than were borrowers. Loan contractions led to occasional bankruptcies and bank failures, which for the most part were well contained. But the panics were brief and did not interfere with long-term economic growth. They typically followed the onset of recessions and did not cause them. Moreover, the costs of the panics in terms of bank failures, depositor losses, or lost output were relatively minor.[8] If anything, the panics infused markets with a renewed sense of caution and conservatism. Overall, of course, the national banking era coincided with a period of unprecedented growth and prosperity for the country. Banks played a significant role in financing the post-Civil War economic expansion, supporting it on footings of sound money and credit.

Although banks were more liquid on an absolute basis during the national banking era than they are today, a relatively greater portion of their reserves were kept in the form of deposits at other banks than was held directly in their own vaults. In particular, in the spring and summer, agricultural banks in rural areas tended to keep reserve balances on deposit at correspondent banks located in cities, primarily in New York. This arrangement explains the seasonal nature of the liquidity crises that were occasionally suffered. In the spring and fall months, agricultural banks would draw on their deposits at city banks to meet higher currency demand associated with planting (spring) and harvesting (fall) activities (Sprague 1910, 19–20; Chari 1989, 11). At other times these interbank deposits were held in New York banks, which typically invested them in call loans —loans to acquire securities. The city banks often paid interest to rural banks for these deposits, because competition compelled them to pass along the interest they could earn by investing the deposits in call loans.

Although these call loans were normally considered liquid and a worthy use of short-term demand deposits, banks found it quite difficult to liquidate them en masse when the fall crop was a healthy one and rural bank withdrawals were heavy. Moreover, the call loans themselves were said to contribute to speculative price rises on stock exchanges, creating inflated values that were not supportable when liquidity was withdrawn. Loan defaults often followed, disrupting business, but the process was seen as a cleansing mechanism as well. Excesses were liquidated and did not accumulate into potentially greater problems in the future.

The liquidity crises of the nineteenth-century U.S. banking system were not an inevitable consequence of unregulated banking. Instead, they were a direct result of distortive interventions in the banking system imposed by government through the national banking acts. These interventions, discussed at length below, included reserve requirements, branching restrictions, and bond-collateral restrictions on currency issuance.

These legal restrictions fostered illiquidity in the banking system in two important ways. First, minimum reserve requirements actually made it impossible for banks to use those reserves for redemption purposes. The intent behind minimum reserve ratios was to ensure bank liquidity, but the exact opposite result was achieved. Only reserves in excess of minimum reserve requirements actually could be used to meet deposit withdrawals. Thus, even if a central reserve city bank met its reserve requirement, it faced a reduction of that ratio (and a violation of the banking laws) with every marginal request for deposit redemption. To preserve or restore its reserve ratio in the face of such withdrawals, it had to build reserves either by acquiring additional reserves or by contracting loans. Ironically, because the actual reserves on hand were just sufficient to meet regulatory liquidity requirements, they could not be used directly to meet demands for liquidity. Of course, this perversity is common to all minimum reserve requirements. Precisely those reserves that are required for liquidity are not available to meet depositor requests for liquidity. Unrestricted by rigid reserve requirements, the banks would have been in a far better position to meet rising demands for liquidity. During this time, the United States was the only major country in the world that had legal reserve requirements (Friedman and Schwartz 1963, 118 note 44).

Second, by segregating the banking system into "country banks," "reserve city banks," and "central reserve city banks," the reserve requirements imposed by government under the national banking system encouraged an unstable inverted "pyramid of reserves" that was susceptible to breakdown during sharp, seasonal variations in the demand for liquidity.[9] Country banks were required to maintain reserves equivalent to 15% of their deposits, two-fifths of which had to be held as cash in their vaults. The rest could be held as deposits at reserve city banks, which typically earned interest. In turn, reserve city banks, located in fifteen designated cities, had to maintain reserves equal to 25% of deposit liabilities, half of which could be held as deposits in central reserve city banks, primarily large New

York City banks. Finally, the central reserve city banks were required to maintain minimum reserve ratios of 25%. The central reserve city banks tended to invest their correspondent balances in call loans, normally the most liquid investment available. When crops were harvested in the fall and the country banks demanded cash, New York banks were forced to meet the withdrawals of interbank deposits by demanding payment on call loans. Had country banks not been encouraged by the National Currency Acts to hold reserves as deposits in reserve city banks, they would have been better equipped to control their own reserves and to satisfy directly seasonal changes in demand for cash. New York banks would have had little reason to invest their funds in call loans.

Branching restrictions imposed by law also encouraged reserve pyramiding by preventing country banks from being branches of banks with head offices in financial centers. Banks with widespread branching networks would have been able to shift reserves flexibly to branches where the demand for cash was greatest, instead of relying on the capacity of other banks to meet requests for cash in a pinch. Branching restrictions also prevented banks from diversifying their assets, a pervasive source of instability that plagues our system even today. Again, the United States was the only major country in the world to impose such onerous branching restrictions.

The illiquidity inherent in the national banking system was also a direct consequence of the bond-collateral provisions spelled out in national legislation. Banks could only issue bank notes, or currency, if the notes were secured by bonds issued by the federal government. The basic purpose of the collateral provision, as Secretary of the Treasury Samuel Chase made clear, was to assist the Union government in financing the Civil War by fostering a demand for its debt. But the provision was also promoted as a way to provide a "uniform" currency and to protect noteholders against ultimate loss—two "public interest" rationalizations that have been interpreted sympathetically by historians.

Whatever the motives of government, the legal restrictions imposed on bank currency fostered illiquidity by making the note issues of banks "inelastic." Banks could not freely expand and contract their note circulation in accordance with the needs of trade, but instead were confined to issuing notes in accordance with the exigencies of government finance. This meant that banks could not easily satisfy shifts in the public's ratio of deposits to currency. The restrictions became ever more onerous as the national banking era progressed, because the U.S. Treasury was reducing the total national debt available to collateralize bank notes in anticipation of resuming specie payments in 1879. Even after resumption, the supply of required collateral was diminishing, especially relative to trade. The relative scarcity put a premium on eligible bond collateral, making note issue excessively costly (Smith 1936, 149). There were also burdensome administrative delays imposed by the Treasury when it approved and shipped out currency, delays that were most binding when the demand for currency was greatest and the state of panic most acute (Horwitz 1990, 640–41).

The money panics of the nineteenth century did not reflect a lack of confidence in banks by depositors but only the fact that it was illegal for bankers to freely meet shifts in depositors' demand for currency relative to checking deposits. As Friedman and Schwartz (1963, 295, note 77) have argued, the panics of the national banking era "resulted much less from the absence of elasticity of the total stock of money than from the absence of interconvertibility of deposits and currency." A system of free banking would have delivered superior results. As George Selgin (1988b, 626) has expained:

> When banks are unrestricted in their ability to issue bank notes, each institution can meet increases in its clients' demands for currency without difficulty and without affecting its liquidity or solvency. . . . The supply of currency is flexible under unrestricted note issue because bank note liabilities are, for a bank capable of issuing them, not significantly different from deposit liabilities. . . . The issue of notes in exchange for deposits merely involves offsetting adjustments on the liability side of the the bank's balance sheet, with no change on the asset side.

Unfortunately, the national banking laws did not permit unrestricted note issue, and therefore banks were forced to meet increased currency demand by paying out reserves and making painful adjustments to their loan assets. Had banks been able to issue notes without inflexible bond-collateral provisions, and with only the requirement that the notes be redeemed in a medium mutually agreed to by bank and noteholder, there would have been no system-wide liquidity crises to speak of in these decades.

Bankers were innovative in trying to offset the perverse effects of these legal restrictions on currency issuance. Sometimes they permitted their reserve ratios to fall temporarily below the 25% legal minimums in order to meet depositor withdrawals and prevent suspensions. The banks would restore their ratios once the stringency passed. In addition, in each of the panics the clearinghouses of central reserve city banks created "clearinghouse certificates" that were used in place of currency to settle reserve clearings between members, thereby preserving the more limited supply of currency needed to meet depositor withdrawals (Timberlake 1984; Gorton 1984). In other cases, bankers and businesses simply issued private currency, bypassing banking laws (Andrew 1908). As a last resort, convertibility was restricted or suspended for brief periods (but only in the panics of 1873, 1893, and 1907) (Gorton 1985). By all these measures, banks were able to minimize the contraction of loans that otherwise would have been necessary to meet withdrawals. But despite the role played by legal restrictions in fostering illiquidity and other distortions in the nineteenth-century banking system, and despite the innovative attempts by banks to overcome these distortions, the banks themselves were largely blamed for the crises. They were condemned as lawbreakers for going below minimum reserve requirements. City banks especially were blamed for paying interest on deposits, for luring country banks into opening correspondent accounts, for financing speculation, and for issuing "unauthorized currency" in the form of clearinghouse certificates.

Government reports implied that fraud, mismanagement, and bank failures were the prime causes of the money panics. In one report, for example, the comptroller of the currency said the 1873 crisis was caused by the payment of interest on deposits and by the financing of speculation by banks. The comptroller (quoted by Sprague 1910, 81) further blamed the few banks that failed during the crisis for having started it, and said the failures were due to "the criminal mismanagement of their officers or to the neglect or violation of the national bank act on the part of their directors." One of the "criminal violations" referred to involved lowering reserve ratios below legal minimums to meet withdrawals. The comptroller, John Jay Knox, simply dismissed the complaint of bankers that legal reserve requirements made those reserves unavailable to depositors, insisting instead that "the provision requiring that a reserve shall be kept on hand at all times was intended to protect the depositor and to keep the bank in funds for the purpose of responding at all times to the demands of its creditors." To suggest that the requirement was harmful, he said, "is equivalent to declaring that the national currency act was intended to provide for the destruction of the very institutions it created."[10] The comptroller recommended increased government intervention into banking: closer scrutiny of bank lending practices, prohibitions on the payment of interest on deposits, and swift prosecution of banks that violate minimum reserve requirements.

Government officials generally did not criticize the reserve requirements, the reserve pyramiding, or the note issuance restrictions imposed under the national banking laws. Where criticisms were voiced, they were not sufficiently adopted to reform the laws. In its report on the crisis of 1873, the Treasury recognized that "with a fixed amount of circulation of bank notes and of United States legal-tender notes not redeemable in coin and with gold above par with currency, there must be each year times of redundancy and times of scarcity of currency, depending wholly on demand, no method existing for increasing the supply. With a circulating medium redeemable in coin, a redundancy is corrected by the export, and a scarcity by the import of specie from other countries." On the basis of this insight, the Treasury recommended "a permanent return to the sound basis of specie payments and a gold standard to which all our paper issues shall be made of equal value."[11] A specie resumption act was passed in 1875 and the United States resumed specie payments on legal tender notes in 1879. The absolute ceiling on aggregate national bank note circulation was lifted and bond-collateral requirements were eased very slightly in 1900. But the main features contributing to illiquidity persisted, and money panics remained a near certainty.

The 1893 panic stemmed not from banker wrongdoing but from uncertainty over the federal government's willingness and ability to maintain the gold standard in the face of pressure from silver interests and other inflationists (Friedman and Schwartz 1963, 104–118). Once uncertainty set in, the destabilizing features of the national banking system outlined above made the situation worse. This time, remarkably, both the comptroller of the currency and the U.S. Treasury Department advocated the repeal of the bond-collateral provisions in their 1894 annual reports. Treasury Secretary Carlisle (quoted in Friedman and Schwartz 1963, 117–18, note 44) went further and even recommended the repeal of legal reserve requirements, arguing that

> every prudent bank, if left free to conduct its deposit and discount business in the manner most advantageous to its own interests and the interests of its patrons, will undoubtedly keep on hand a reasonable reserve to meet not only all the ordinary demands upon it, but to provide for such emergencies as are liable to occur . . . but it ought not be prohibited by law from using

such reserve for the only purposes it was designed to accomplish. . . . To provide for a reserve which can not be utilized even at a time of greatest stringency and distrust without incurring penalties of forfeiture, affords a most striking illustration of the impolicy of legislative interference with the natural laws of trade and finance.

Unfortunately, the insights and recommendations of the Treasury were ignored by legislatures, bankers were again blamed for the panic, and the destabilizing "legislature interference" recognized by Secretary Carlisle remained in place.

The panic of 1907 was the last of the money panics under the national banking era, but it was the most important because it was a precursor to passage of the still more interventionist Federal Reserve Act. The exact origins of the panic are widely debated still today. Sprague's authoritative account has demonstrated the considerable financial strength and prudent lending postures of the reserve city and central reserve city banks prior to the crisis, so there is little reason to suspect speculative influences played a major role (Sprague 1910, 216–24). "But there was another influence," remarked Sprague (1910, 230–31), "potent during this period, which tended positively to encourage unsound banking—a large government surplus." In and of itself, a surplus reflected sound public finance. But the surplus meant that government securities, required to back bank currency, were in short supply. As before, seasonal instability set in, and the reserve pyramid started to topple. This time, trying to overcome the illiquidity that ensued, Secretary of the Treasury Shaw engaged in a series of disruptive operations, depositing and then suddenly withdrawing government deposits from banks in need of cash (Sprague 1910, 230–32). His efforts to manage the equivalent of a game of musical chairs were futile, if not destabilizing.

Congress further undermined confidence in financial markets in the summer of 1907, when it conducted hostile investigations of the railroad and mining industries in keeping with the age of "trust-busting" and the wishes of President Theodore Roosevelt (Groseclose 1980, 16–25). This, in turn, led to the failure of some trust companies, notably Knickerbocker Trust Company, due to falling securities values. Unlike the banks, trust companies had a disproportionate share of assets in securities and call loans, making them more vulnerable; meanwhile, only six banks failed during the panic (Calomiris and Gorton 1991, 157). Nevertheless, after the impact of the securities losses, the 1907 panic snowballed for reasons not terribly different from those in earlier panics. Legal restrictions prevented banks from satisfying changes in the deposit/currency ratio, when fall crops started to move. Again, bankers tried to respond by resorting to clearinghouse certificates and emergency currency.

Banks ran the risk of being charged with breaking the law for issuing "unauthorized" currency (Horwitz 1990, 641–43). But government officials could not ignore the effectiveness of the issues in ameliorating the 1907 Panic, and legalized the procedure via the Aldrich-Vreeland Act of 1908 (otherwise known as the "Emergency Currency Act"). The act effectively "decriminalized" the issuance of emergency currency, selectively permitting groups of banks to issue currency, when needed, on the basis of usual banking assets, not government bonds. The act was only intended as a temporary measure, and emergency currency was only allowed to supplement, not replace, the bond-based currency already in circulation. Nevertheless, the concept behind the Aldrich-Vreeland Act proved eminently successful on the one occasion when it was relied upon before the Federal Reserve was formed. The beginnings of a liquidity panic, resulting from the outbreak of World War I in the summer of 1914, were blocked by the issuance of $400 million in emergency currency, representing nearly one-quarter of total currency in the hands of the public after issue. When anxieties diminished, the currency was withdrawn and retired. According to Friedman and Schwartz (1963, 172, 693–94), the act "provided an effective device for solving a threatened interconvertibility crisis without monetary contraction or widespread bank failures." In fact, they contend that the experience of the summer of 1914 showed that the Aldrich-Vreeland Act alone was capable of preventing future panics, that a Federal Reserve was unnecessary, and that emergency currency powers available to the private banking system would have been sufficient even to forestall the 1929–33 crisis.[12]

Despite distortions imposed by government under national banking laws, and the innovative solutions of private bankers to overcome those distortions, the banking community was made a scapegoat for the 1907 crisis, and additional government intervention was recommended. Congress initiated two full-scale investigations to achieve these purposes. First, acting on a requirement of the Aldrich-Vreeland Act, it formed the National Monetary Commission to study the prospects for reforming the banking system. The commission published over twenty volumes applauding the alleged virtues of foreign central banking systems, clearly pushing a foregone conclusion. Although the commission formally recommended a "private" solution (incorporating a National Reserve Association among banks in the United States) to currency panics, its predominantly favorable views on central banks abroad, and its inability to fully recognize and advise repeal of the interventionist defects of the national banking laws, paved the way for the creation of what has turned out to be a powerful central bank, the Federal Reserve, in 1913.

A major impetus to establishing the Fed, however, came from another congressional committee bent on making bankers the scapegoats. The House Committee on Banking and Currency convened a subcommittee in April 1912 "to investigate the concentration of money and credit" in private hands (Cleveland and Huertas 1985, 67). Chaired by Louisiana Representative Arsene Pujo, and in operation through February 1913, the "Pujo Committee" lambasted Wall Street banks for conducting an allegedly abusive, clandestine, and conspiratorial "money trust," supposedly to the detriment of sound banking, market liquidity, and the economy at large. After months of investigation the Pujo Committee concluded that five firms—J. P. Morgan, First National Bank, National City Bank, Guaranty Trust Company, and Bankers Trust Company—had interlocking directorships in various financial and industrial companies with total capital of $22 billion (Cleveland and Huertas 1985, 67, 359 note 53, 360 note 54). The growth of these banks, and their relationships, reflected the massive growth in the country's industrial base, and the need to pull together a legislatively fragmented banking structure (Chernow 1990, 153). But they were suspected of wrongdoing all the same, even though the committee never proved that such relationships caused or worsened the periodic money panics or instabilities of the pre-Fed era. The committee did claim, incredibly, that city banks may have purposely starved country banks of liquidity at crucial times. Of course, the committee ignored the basic illegality of meeting currency demand under national bank laws, and it made no attempt to reconcile its charge with the opposite conclusion contained in a report of the National Monetary Commission, that city banks had caused panics by overly favoring the country banks with attractive correspondent services (see Sprague 1910). Publicity rather than objectivity appears to have been the major consideration of these reformers and other "trust-busters" at the turn of the century.

Animosity toward private bankers was common among politicians. In debate over the Federal Reserve Act, Senator Hitchcock (quoted in Timberlake 1989, 5) expressed the prevailing sentiment against concentrations of power, except in the hands of government: "We believe in government control, real and actual, all the time," he said, "and we do not believe that the banking interests in any community should be entrusted with that power." Presidential candidate Woodrow Wilson (quoted in Cleveland and Huertas 1985, 67), in one bit of tortured logic, claimed that "Wall Street brought on the 1907 Panic, got the people to demand currency reform, brought the Aldrich-Vreeland currency bill forward and, if it dares, will produce another panic to pass the Aldrich central bank plan. We need reform," he urged, "but not at the hands of Wall Street." He also (Cleveland and Huertas 1985, 360 note 55; Chernow 1990, 149) called the Wall Street banking community "the most dangerous of all monopolies," and said, "a concentration of the control of credit . . . may at any time become infinitely dangerous to free enterprise" —a warning not against proposals for a central bank but against private banks.

As president two years later, Wilson would sign the bill forming the Federal Reserve, granting the government itself monopoly powers over money and credit in the United States. He did so even though Wall Street did not produce the panic he expected; in fact, as mentioned above, private banks positively suppressed a panic caused by government declarations of war. The momentum for increased intervention was fueled by the tendency (common on later occasions as well) for leading bankers to appease their critics in politics and the media and even to assist Congress in drafting laws bringing further intervention to the industry.[13]

While there were a few insightful contemporary critics of the national banking system (e.g., Noyes 1910), most reformers unfortunately did not recognize the benefits of free branching, unrestricted note issue, and decentralized reserve management. They correctly saw panics as reflecting an "inelastic currency," but somehow blamed bankers instead of the law for their inability to manage the currency properly. Instead of freeing the note issue, they recommended that government nationalize the note issue. Instead of repealing the inherent rigidities of the national banking laws, they condemnned the alleged inordinate concentration of financial resources and management in a few, inept, private hands, and called for its concentration in still fewer, albeit government, hands, at the Federal Reserve. Instead of having the control of capital in Wall Street, they demanded that control be shifted to Washington. They apparently had no conception that much greater ineptitude might follow such a shift. Failing to locate the underlying source of nineteenth-century U.S. banking panics in the distortive interventions of the national banking laws, reformers erected a superstructure of central banking that would eventually prove more destabilizing.

IV. The Banking Crisis of the 1930s and the Expansion of Federal Reserve Powers

The stock market crash of 1929, the banking crisis of 1931–1933, and the Great Depression suffered in the 1930s were disasters of unprecedented proportion in the history of U.S. finance. Nearly one-third of all banks failed. Legal restrictions on banks that prevented branching and the diversification of risks meant that most failures were of small, single-office banks tied by law to undiversified pockets of the economy. Legal prohibitions on private note issue were also harmful, as neither banks nor clearinghouse associations were permitted to issue currency to meet depositor claims. The economic impact of the banking collapse was profoundly damaging, as the money supply and income fell by a third, business investment plummeted, and unemployment reached 25%.

The basic cause of the banking crisis was the Fed's monopoly on the issuance of money and its attendant power to manipulate money and credit in defiance of market preferences. Erratic inflations of the money supply by the Fed in the 1920s encouraged the real estate and stock market speculation for which that decade became known (Rothbard 1975, 126–52). To foster monetary inflation, the Fed had actively countered the long-established, conservative rules of the gold standard. Instead of tightening monetary policy in response to gold outflows (which signaled relatively higher prices in the United States than in foreign countries), the Fed chose to replace its gold holdings with government debt instruments, in the process loosening monetary policy at precisely the wrong time.[14] The Fed decelerated its inflating in 1928, and the stock market crashed the following year. By gross mismanagement of system liquidity in the following four years, the Fed brought on the collapse of the banking system, and the Great Depression (Friedman and Schwartz 1963, chapter 7). The Fed had supposedly been established as a better alternative to the speculations of private bankers and as a means of providing an elastic currency to prevent banking panics, but on both counts it failed blatantly. In the 1920s, it supplied too much money and fostered speculation and unsound lending, while in the crisis of the 1930s it supplied too little currency and failed to satisfy a large-scale shift in depositors' demand for currency.[15]

As a monopoly issuer of currency, the Fed's performance was universally destructive, for without the Fed's monopoly, the market would have had no unilateral source of speculative excess, and in troubled times could have turned to more reliable providers of currency. A fully free, private banking system would not have been wholly free of mistakes, but neither would the entire system be exposed to unilateral mismanagement of a government agency, as it was under central banking. The proper response to this disaster would have been to limit sharply (or abolish) the Federal Reserve, return gold and the management of the gold standard to the private banking system, eliminate reserve requirements, permit the issuance of currency by banks (this time without bond collateral provisions), and repeal branching restrictions. But because the proper cause of the crisis was not identified, wholly opposite reforms were enacted. As in earlier crises, a congressional commission was formed that made the bankers scapegoats and laid the foundation for still greater grants of legislative power to the Federal Reserve and other banking regulatory agencies. Among other things, the Pecora Commission (named for the legal counsel to the Senate Banking Committee, Ferdinand Pecora) condemned bankers for promoting speculations, stock price manipulation, and fraud. The commission charged that private bankers caused the collapse of their own industry in particular and of economic activity in general.

The Pecora Commission set the moral tone for the banking reforms of the 1930s. The commission did not engage in dispassionate analysis of the banking industry or government policies, nor did it explore remedies in any scientific manner. Rather, its hearings were infused with indignation against the banking community, charging that it had worked in near-conspiratorial manner to bust the stock market, bring down banks, and wreck the economy. Its emotion-laden bias colored the legislation that was passed during and soon after the hearings. Although other, more dispassionate sessions were conducted around the time of the Pecora hearings, the damage inflicted on the reputation and credibility of the financial community by the commission made it easier for lawmakers to justify comprehensive interventionist reforms.[16] Senator Carter Glass, chairman of the Senate Banking and Currency Committee, conducted hearings that eventually brought legislation separating commercial and investment banking. As one writer (Flannery 1985, 69) contends, the Pecora hearings "became a watershed in Glass's drive to divorce investment banking from deposit banking in the United States."

The Pecora hearings focused on National City Bank, its chairman Charles Mitchell, and its brokerage affiliate, National City Company, charging not only that they engaged in financial malpractice and fraud but also that such activity was representative of the entire financial community and responsible for the stock market crash, the banking collapse, and the Depression. This broad charge was never substantiated, and the fact that National City and bankers were scapegoats was clear, even to Pecora. He later admitted to picking Mitchell as his lead witness not because of suspicions of wrongdoing but because "National City was one of the very largest banks in the world, and had but recently been surpassed by the Chase National. The prestige and reputation of these institutions was enormous. They stood, in the mind of the financially unsophisticated public, for safety, strength, prudence, and high-mindedness, and they were supposed to be captained by men of unimpeachable integrity, possessing almost mythical business genius and foresight" (Pecora 1939, 71). Instead of simply assuming that the banks' sterling reputation was wholly undeserved, Pecora and his fellow congressional investigators might better have considered that bankers would not wish to throw such an asset away in a suicidal flourish.

The Pecora Report charged that National City's securities affiliate failed to disclose material facts, pursued high-pressure sales tactics, traded in the stock of National City Bank, obtained customer referrals from the bank, and took bad loans off the books of the bank (Kelly 1985, 52). Importantly, the Pecora hearings did not show that these practices weakened the bank or its affiliate, or in any way contributed to the general crisis.[17] In fact, with a historical perspective devoid of the emotionalism of the time, these practices appear relatively innocuous. Although Pecora's charges referred to technical matters, the message to the public was that a grand immorality had been perpetrated. The public took the message to heart. One historian (Chernow 1990, 356) recalls that "as people followed the hearings on their farms and in their offices, on soup lines and in Hoovervilles, they became convinced that they'd been conned in the 1920s. Yesterday's gods were no more than greedy little devils." Another writer (Flannery 1985, 70–71) observes that the "publicity surrounding National City Bank chairman Charles Mitchell's testimony generated widespread and intense public reaction. Bankers came to be viewed as venal, selfish, and perhaps responsible for the depression." A history of the National City Bank (Cleveland and Huertas 1985, 172) recounts that "as crisis followed crisis and the depression deepened, the public mood darkened. Shock and dismay gave way to anger and bitterness and a need to assign blame. Wall Street bankers became the object of the public's mounting wrath." Media coverage contributed to the search for scapegoats: "as the depression deepened, the press increasingly pictured banks as villains rather than victims. Bankers, Charles Mitchell foremost among them, were reviled as 'banksters' " (Cleveland and Huertas 1985, 160).

These hostile images of bankers were reinforced in Congress by politicians like Senator Wheeler of Montana, who said (quoted in Cleveland and Huertas 1985, 356), "The best way to restore confidence in the banks would be to take these crooked presidents out of the banks and treat them the same way we treated Al Capone when he failed to pay his income tax." When the most respected banker of the day, J.P. Morgan, Jr., was brought before the Pecora Commission, he was primarily ridiculed for having paid no income tax in the previous three years (Cleveland and Huertas 1985, 366). No evidence was uncovered to suggest that his bank or its syndicates had caused the crisis. Instead, the commission criticized the Morgan bank for what could as easily have been interpreted as its business success, namely, its extensive dealings with the country's top companies, and for its prominent role as a "bankers' bank." The vilification of the bankers extended right up to the White House. In his first inaugural address in 1933, President Roosevelt (quoted in Cleveland and Huertas 1985, 190) blamed the crisis on the country's leading bankers, and referred to them as "the unscrupulous money-changers" who "through their own stubbornness and incompetence, have admitted their failure, and have abdicated . . . from their high seats in the temple of civilization." With criticism of bankers coming from every quarter—Congress, the White House, the media, and the public—the punitive system of banking regulation enacted in the 1930s was inevitable.

The most respected academic expert on banking at the time, H. Parker Willis of Columbia University (quoted in Flannery 1985, 71), took a different view:

> A fair examination of the facts disclosed by the Senate investigation leaves the feeling that but few persons, relatively, have been examined, and that these, while often "prominent" are not in themselves representative of

either banking or business. We must, accordingly, reject entirely the notion that—so far as these inquiries show—there has been a revelation of demonstrated crookedness on the part of American finance, trade, and banking at large. There has been nothing of the sort.

Willis was the principal advisor to Senator Glass on legislative reforms, but his assessment was ignored by Glass, who was instrumental in giving greater powers to government banking agencies after the crisis. The fact that neither Willis nor the politicians he advised in the 1930s placed much blame for the crisis on the central bank may be explained by the fact that both Willis and Glass had also played key roles in the drafting of the Federal Reserve Act in 1913.[18]

Other congressional hearings in the 1930s focused more on the poor lending experience of lenders (such as that of National City Bank in Latin America) and less on bankers' moral turpitude. But the bankers were blamed nonetheless. Senator Couzens of Michigan (quoted in Cleveland and Huertas 1985, 185) claimed that "unreasonable salaries and bonuses lead to unsound banking and unsound sales of securities." Bankers were criticized for their paychecks, for financing real estate and stock speculations, for supporting securities affiliates with commercial loans, and for being insufficiently liquid to survive depositor runs on their institutions. Private depositors were criticized for wanting to convert their deposits or for "hoarding" gold. But there was virtually no criticism of the Federal Reserve for its inflation of money and credit in the 1920s, or for its mismanagement of the discount window in the early 1930s. There was also no criticism of the regulatory restrictions on branching that prevented diversification and kept many banks small and vulnerable to failure.

Some congresspeople, eager to pin the blame for the crisis on private bankers, claimed that the small percentage of commercial banks with securities affiliates had caused each of the important disasters, from the stock market crash to the banking collapse to the Great Depression. Senator Glass, in sponsoring legislation forceably separating commercial and investment banking, declared, "These affiliates were the most unscrupulous contributors, next to the debauch of the New York Stock Exchange, to the financial catastrophe which visited this country and were mainly responsible for the depression under which we have been suffering since. They ought speedily to be separated from the parent and in this bill we have done that" (77 *Congressional Record*, 19 May 1933, 3726).

The separation was finalized in the Banking Act passed in June 1933.

The facts about the role of securities activities in commercial bank failures do not support Glass's view. First, commercial banks had been involved in the securities business, through brokerage subsidiaries, well before the 1920s.[19] Second, fewer than 8% of the national banks with the biggest securities operations failed during the crisis, while over 26% of all national banks failed. More important, most failures involved smaller state banks that did not conduct securities businesses. Finally, in many cases the presence of securities affiliates actually reduced the probability of bank failure (White 1986). Even in the few cases where banks were found to have failed due to a fall in security values, economist William F. Shughart, II (1988, 605) has argued that "it is disingenuous to accuse bankers of bad management after the fact when unanticipated events have caused the realized rate of return on a particular asset to be less than expected." In short, the securities activities of commercial banks were not responsible for the stock market crash, the banking crisis, or the depression (Flannery 1985). Reformers nevertheless played on the sensationalism of these events and pinned blame squarely on bankers.

In passing the Glass-Steagall Act, Congress was able to divide and conquer the banking industry. Brokerage firms would have a protected securities market all to themselves, and commercial banks would not face competition from brokerage firms taking deposits. Passage was assured once bankers tried to appease the politicians. In March 1933, after much criticism, National City Bank and Chase National Bank agreed voluntarily to divest their securities affiliates, and the American Bankers Association, after early opposition, also caved in to pressure and supported the act.[20] Before it was also targeted, J. P. Morgan's bank had applauded the actions of President Roosevelt, especially his demolition of the gold standard.[21] The U.S. Treasury also benefited by the act because it purged commercial bank portfolios of private securities, which increasingly had competed with government securities for loanable funds in the 1920s (Shughart 1988, 600, 610–11).

The money and banking reforms that were adopted in the 1930s reflected entirely the misconceptions about what had caused the crisis. Instead of reining in or abolishing the Fed, Congress granted it still greater powers, including the centralization of power at the

Board of Governors in Washington. Instead of removing political motives associated with Fed policymaking, the Glass-Steagall Act permitted the Fed to back its issues of currency with government debt, whereas in the original Federal Reserve Act it had to back them with commercial paper and gold (Friedman and Schwartz 1963, 191, note 4). Instead of returning the supply of gold and the management of the gold standard to the private banking system, the government criminalized the private ownership of gold, confiscated gold holdings of banks and citizens, abrogated the gold clauses of Treasury bond indentures, and devalued the dollar.[22] Instead of giving banks the power to issue currency and satisfy the changing preferences of the public for currency relative to deposits, the government gave the Fed a virtually unlimited capacity to issue money. Instead of permitting banks to become safer through free branching and the diversification of loans and deposits, it erected a system of government deposit insurance to "guarantee" deposits. In the process, flat-rate "insurance" assessments were imposed on banks that effectively taxed prudent institutions for the benefit of reckless ones. Even Franklin Roosevelt (1938, 37) recognized at the time that federal deposit insurance "would put a premium on unsound banking in the future." Instead of leaving banks free to make credit decisions on a sound basis, the Fed and other banking agencies assumed greater influence over bank lending policies, and forceably separated commercial and investment banking. On the pretext that bad lending flowed inevitably from the payment of interest on deposits, government imposed ceilings on the rates banks offered. Finally, instead of abolishing reserve requirements, government actually raised them in the mid-1930s, precipitating a second depression in 1937–1938.

In every respect, government interventions in money and banking were expanded and intensified in the early 1930s, despite the sorry record of interventionism. This result was made possible by a diversion of attention, by intense muckraking investigations of private banking activities, and by the virtual absolution of all government sins associated with the crisis. The work of the Pecora Commission positioned private bankers as scapegoats for a government-created crisis and provided justifications for ensuing legislation. The reforms that were passed did not solve the fundamental problems associated with central banking and legal restrictions, but only further undermined sound money and banking.

V. Institutionalized Inflation and the Deterioration of Banking in the Postwar Period, 1945–1980

Compared to the instability of today, the money and banking system appeared quite stable in the postwar decades leading up to the banking reforms of the early 1980s. But closer examination reveals that these decades were characterized by prolonged and profound deterioration. The money and banking reforms of the 1930s set the stage for an unprecedented wave of inflation that began building after World War II and accelerated in the 1960s and 1970s, encouraging speculative lending practices at thrifts and commercial banks. These decades were marred by chronic deficit spending and inflation, both of which were made possible by the fiat money-creating power of the Federal Reserve, power that had been significantly enhanced in the reforms of the 1930s. In addition, during these decades interest rates were high and volatile, reflecting inflation expectations, and exposing banks and thrifts to damaging maturity mismatches.

The postwar commercial banking system in the United States suffered a secular deterioration in its financial condition that closely mirrored the ongoing debasement of the dollar. For example, the aggregate capital ratio of the banking system declined from over 14% at the end of the Great Depression to under 7% in the early 1980s (Salsman 1990, 52–75). Other measures of financial performance in the banking industry—such as asset quality, profitability, and liquidity—showed similarly grim trends. Boom-and-bust patterns, such as the real estate debacle of the mid-1970s, appeared quite similar to those of the 1920s. As the credit ratings of banks fell below those of top customers, banks lost sound lending business to the commercial paper market and floundered to make up the difference with loans against real estate, to the stock market, to Socialist foreign governments, highly leveraged companies, and overextended consumers. On the liability side, banks suffered a massive outflow of depositor funds to relatively unregulated money market mutual funds, a process of "disintermediation" made possible by a combination of inflation (causing high rates) and legal ceilings on bank deposit interest rates (Regulation Q). By the late 1970s, banks were fleeing the Federal Reserve system to escape the costs of maintaining reserves (which paid no interest) and losing deposits.

S&Ls were even worse off than banks, straining under inflation rates and interest rates that reached as high as 14.5% and 21.5%, respectively, in the late 1970s. The Fed's inflationist policies proved destructive to the S&Ls, whose business consisted of making long-term fixed rate home mortgages funded by short-term savings deposits. When interest rates increased, S&Ls could not reprice their assets quickly enough to reflect new market yields. They also suffered from disintermediation, along with banks. In 1979 alone, when Treasury Bill rates were as much as 6% above permissible bank rates, savings accounts at banks and thrifts fell by over $12 billion.

This prolonged postwar deterioration in money and banking—culminating in the "dollar crisis" of the late 1970s—was made possible by the government's fiat money monopoly, the widespread acceptance of Keynesian economics, and the chronic deficit spending and inflationism that resulted from both. Following the inflation of the 1960s, the last link of gold to the dollar (convertible for foreign central banks) was severed in 1971, ushering in still higher rates of inflation thereafter. Few of the difficulties suffered by banks and thrifts would have arisen had government not sponsored inflation and interest rate controls.

Unfortunately, popular explanations for postwar deterioration in money and banking blamed bankers, not government. Inflation and high interest rates were blamed not on the money monopolist, the Federal Reserve, but on greedy businesspeople and bankers. The dollar crisis was blamed on "international speculators," instead of on the sole issuer of dollars, the Fed.[23] Disintermediation was blamed on "competitive pressures" emanating from the relatively unregulated mutual fund industry, whose accounts paid market rates of interest. Banks were blamed for leaving the Federal Reserve System and making it difficult to conduct monetary policy. They were blamed for creating holding companies, even though these were devised to overcome branching and business line restrictions, in order to diversify income sources. They were criticized when they tried to achieve efficiencies through mergers; for example, the merger of Manufacturers Trust and the Hanover Bank faced four years of regulatory obstacles in the early 1960s. Banks were blamed for speculative lending, and S&Ls were blamed for lending long while borrowing short, even though government housing credit agencies had encouraged them to do so.

By failing again to properly identify the cause of the postwar deterioration in money and banking, government once again enacted reforms that failed to solve the basic problems inherent in central banking and instead provided the impetus for the further deterioration we are experiencing today. Instead of permitting a greater variety of income sources, Congress passed the Bank Holding Company Act in 1956 to restrict banks' well-intentioned diversification strategies. Instead of discouraging overcapacity and encouraging cost efficiencies, the Justice Department and federal courts blocked or delayed the bank mergers that would make them possible. Instead of encouraging diversification, the 1970 Douglas Amendment to the Bank Holding Company Act placed limits on branching. Instead of abandoning Federal Reserve inflationism when the dollar weakened in the late 1960s, President Nixon abandoned the international gold standard. Instead of controlling Federal Reserve inflationism in the 1970s, Nixon and Carter both imposed controls during the decade on the symptoms of that policy, ever-rising wages, prices, and credit. Instead of addressing the reasons why banks were fleeing the Federal Reserve System, legislation in 1980 simply required all depository institutions to be members.[24] Instead of addressing the underlying deterioration of banks and thrifts and the diminished confidence of depositors, the 1980 reforms nearly tripled federal insurance coverage, from $40,000 per deposit account to $100,000. The 1980 reforms established a six-year phaseout of deposit interest rate ceilings to address disintermediation, but the business that flowed to the mutual funds never returned, and many institutions were left fatally weakened by the previous controls. The Garn-St. Germain Act of 1982 tried to remedy this weakness by granting thrifts wider lending powers, but the combination of greater latitude in asset choice, together with a massive expansion of the federally insured deposits funding those assets, was a sure prescription for recklessness.

None of the reforms of the early 1980s would have been necessary had blame been properly placed on deficit spending, inflationism, and legal restrictions on banks. The only proper response to the deterioration would have been to identify and eradicate its root cause, central banking and legal restrictions. Government policymakers should have rejected Keynesian-inspired deficit spending policies. They should have restrained or abolished the engine of inflation that is the Federal Reserve. They should have scaled back and ultimately abolished deposit insurance, and permitted full branching, merger, and investment banking powers. Ultimately, they should have denationalized gold and considered the adoption of free banking on a gold standard.

VI. The Present Banking Crisis

If the banking reforms of 1980 and 1982 had attacked the root cause of the banking problem, we would have seen some improvement in the banking system in the rest of the decade. Instead, the deterioration of banks and thrifts accelerated, despite months of unbroken economic growth. The extent of the thrift debacle in the United States is by now well known. Nearly a third of the thirty-one hundred S&Ls in existence in 1980 have since failed or reached insolvency while being propped up by government assistance. Nearly 20% of the $1 trillion of assets in the industry became "nonperforming" in the decade of the 1980s. The industry's deposit insurance fund was depleted in less than four years after reaching a high of $6 billion in 1985. Estimates of the total cost of the S&L debacle have reached $500 billion (or $130 billion on a present value basis over thirty years), and due to legislation passed in 1989, the costs will be borne directly by taxpayers.[25]

There has also been massive deterioration in the commercial banking industry. Since 1980, U.S. banks have failed at rates unseen since the Great Depression. Even in inflation-adjusted terms, the largest bank failures in our history have occurred in the last decade. Whether lending to LDCs, to "leveraged buyouts," or to commercial real estate projects, bankers have made lending mistakes of stupendous proportion in recent decades. Since at least 1984, when it bailed out the failed Continental Illinois, the government has offered a de facto bailout promise to all creditors of those banks it deems "too big to fail," regardless of the detrimental effects of such a policy on sound banking practice. In perhaps the ultimate sign of desperation, the Federal Reserve has been using its discount window to bail out insolvent banks (large and small alike), far beyond its original purpose of providing liquidity.[26] The deposit insurance system for commercial banks has also collapsed. As recently as 1987 the fund of the Federal Deposit Insurance Corporation (FDIC) reached a peak of $18 billion, but was expected to be insolvent by the end of 1991, and in the red by as much as $60 billion in a few years. The ratio of insurance funds to insured deposits, which was never high to begin with, fell gradually from 1.16% in 1980 to .60% at the end of 1990. The burden of this collapse is being shouldered by the more prudent banks that have survived but must now pay higher insurance premiums into the fund. FDIC premium rates have tripled since 1988.

The cumulative burdens placed on the banking system by government inflation, deposit insurance, and branching restrictions have begun to intensify the rate of deterioration of the industry in this decade. Skyrocketing federal budget deficits and the Fed's ongoing commitment to finance them through monetary inflation have contributed significantly to a near doubling of the money supply between 1982 and 1990. By transmitting inflation to the banking system through open-market operations, the Fed has indirectly encouraged reckless lending. The near tripling of deposit insurance coverage has also promoted risk taking by depository institutions. Finally, the continuation of the majority of restrictions on branching has ensured a relatively undiversified mix of bank assets that are therefore prone to downturns in regional economies.

The private banking system is still reeling under the onslaught of central banking. But there is one bank in the United States that has succeeded in resisting this deterioration, that has prospered both in reputation and financial resources with every passing decade, and that has grown to become the largest, most profitable bank in the country. That bank is none other than the Federal Reserve, which earned $24 billion in 1990 alone, on an asset base of approximately $300 billion.[27] These profits far surpass the earnings of all the banks in the United States combined. Moreover, the Fed's rate of return on assets is nearly eight times the level earned by private banks. The "monopolistic concentration of unbridled financial power" that reformers had vilified nearly a century ago has truly come to pass after all these years, and it is ironic to consider that it would not have been possible without their help and the help of their descendents.

As might be expected, popular analysis sees the present current banking crisis as a result not of unbridled Federal Reserve power, but of banker mismanagement, fraud, and "deregulation." A widely publicized study issued by the comptroller of the currency in 1988 concluded, on slim evidence, that mismanagement and fraud were the main causes of modern-day banking failures.[28] In 1990 the U.S. Justice Department reported that more than four hundred people had been convicted of fraud at thrifts in 1988 and 1989, creating losses of $6.4 billion; as troubling as this may appear, it is noteworthy that the loss represents less than 5% of the total estimated loss of the thrift debacle. The Justice Department also reported recently that losses at commercial banks attributable to fraud are lower still than those at thrifts, even though the banking industry is three times as large, and losses from fraud have increased recently.[29]

There is little doubt that the competence and probity of bankers in the United States has deteriorated precipitously throughout this century, whereas bankers were rightly seen as conservative and incorruptible in the nineteenth century, when our system was freer. But the fact remains that a significant portion of the loss associated with today's banking crisis simply is not explained by fraud. Yet government officials have persisted in suggesting otherwise.

Contrary to the claims of a sensationalist media and self-serving regulatory agencies, fraud has not been responsible for the crisis in our banking system, and there is nothing inherent in the business of banking that would necessarily invite it. Fraud is the proximate, not the fundamental cause of bank failure, and failures have been widespread even in the absence of fraud, as in the 1930s. In fact, to the extent that there is greater fraud in banking today, it is positively encouraged by government incentives, such as deposit insurance. Any government that guarantees the liabilities of an entire industry invites the incompetent and the fraudulent, despite all the regulatory efforts expended to resist them. A liability is a promise to deliver some value. If a regime is erected that tends to remove the responsibility for delivering on that promise, those who are irresponsible about meeting promises will necessarily be attracted to it.

More fundamentally, central banking itself institutionalizes unsound and dishonest banking, increasing the likelihood that incompetent, dishonest bankers will be found amidst the rubble of bank failures. Monetary inflation is the most significant form of this institutionalized dishonesty. Wealth does not come from the issuance of paper money. At root, inflation of the money supply constitutes a continuous series of defaults on the part of government, and a highly deceptive means of securing economic resources at the expense of unsuspecting victims. Nonetheless, there are repeated calls for an "easy" monetary policy and a constantly booming economy in which prudent bankers are virtually indistinguishable from those who are incompetent, dishonest, or merely lucky. Deposit insurance goes further still, forcing the prudent to pay the bills of the reckless. In free banking systems, management excellence is rewarded; mismanagement and fraud are minimized, and when they do occur, those harmed by such banks can turn to government courts for justice and remedy. But under central banking, frauds such as inflation are basic components of government policy, and there is no place to turn, certainly not to government, for restitution. Central banking does not insure integrity or competence in money and banking—it actively undermines them by supporting, protecting, and institutionalizing their opposites.

Today's bankers are also charged with gross mismanagement, though there is little evidence that management failings alone have brought on the crisis. A long history of evidence does exist, however, that mismanagement in banking tends to occur in clusters, especially under systems of central banking. Those in the Austrian school of economics, such as Friedrich A. Hayek (1932), have demonstrated how the manipulation of money and credit by government central banks causes widespread malinvestments of economic resources. Policies aimed at artificially lowering the market's "natural" rate of interest makes some economic projects seem more profitable than they would be if the cost of capital were determined in a purely market context. Bank credit skills are undermined in the process; when the central bank inflates and money is easy, it appears that every loan is a good one, and when the central bank tightens, it seems none are good. When money and credit are constantly manipulated by government, bankers find there is an ever-diminishing connection between their lending policies and the success or failure of those policies in practice. By the nature of their work, bankers are unavoidably ensconced in the manipulation of money and credit that surrounds them. They know it best only when they must periodically translate "malinvestment" into "loan losses." The long-term decline in management competence in the banking industry is real, but it is inherent in central banking, not in the banking profession per se.

Banks have found it difficult in recent decades to attract competent management; but notably, it is a difficulty shared only by other industries that are similarly characterized by significant government intervention or protection, such as utilities. Fortunately, most bankers today are competent, conscientious, and honest—as they have been throughout U.S. history. To their credit, they have developed innovative solutions to the inherent instability imposed by central banking. When restrictions imposed on note issue under the National Banking System caused money panics, they developed "clearinghouse certificates" and other forms of private currency that consumers demanded. When restrictions imposed by the Glass-Steagall Act in the 1930s prevented banks from underwriting securities and doing business with the best U.S. companies, they invented term loans. When branching and new product opportunities were blocked by law and narrowly constrained banks in the 1950s, they created holding companies to permit growth and diversification. When interest rate ceilings and restrictions on deposit gathering, together with inflation-driven high interest rates, led to an outflow of deposits in the 1960s and 1970s, they created certificates of deposit and "Eurodollar" accounts. When central banking brought volatility to foreign exchange markets and interest rates in the 1970s and 1980s, they created hedging products to enhance stability. More recently, in response to central banking's double-digit growth rates in money and credit that ballooned bank balance sheets and dwarfed capital, they invented "securitization," the process of preserving liquidity and capital adequacy by packaging loans and selling them in the secondary markets. To the extent that there has been any stability in the banking sector under central banking, it has been achieved by the creative efforts of skilled private bankers—in spite of central banking, not because of it.

Explanations of today's banking crisis that blame "deregulation" are probably the most misguided. The fact is, the commercial banking and thrift industries remain the most regulated sectors of the U.S. economy, and the historical trend has been for government to increase its intervention in these industries—notwithstanding occasional superficial changes in the rules by which the industries must operate. In truth, the argument against "deregulation" simply rests on the mistaken view that banker mismanagement and fraud are responsible for banking instability. Regulation is seen as restraining such impulses, while the relaxation of such restraints is thought to invite fraud and mismanagement. The argument that "deregulation has caused the banking crisis" is simply another way of saying that, left to their own devices in a free or freer environment, bankers will inevitably be incompetent or fraudulent. To blame "deregulation" for banking system deterioration is an unwarranted attempt to resurrect the fallacy that free banking is inherently unstable. That this charge is leveled in today's context—when we have a banking system thoroughly infused with central banking features and legal restrictions—is truly remarkable. That the charge is leveled by influential voices and proposed in legislative chambers is as true today as ever. Lowell Bryan, a prominent bank consultant at McKinsey and Company, has advocated recently that government reimpose controls on deposit interest rates, and legislate lending standards for banks, on the grounds that the banking crisis was caused by banks left free in these areas.[30]

Popular arguments that purport to explain the deterioration of today's banking industry have the case reversed. It is believed that government intervention is the solution to banking instability, whereas in fact it is most assuredly the cause of it. Government intervention has undermined the safety of virtually all banks and S&Ls—and yet critics cite "deregulation" as the problem. Government has created a chaotic monetary environment and a deposit insurance regime that rewards imprudence—and yet blame is directed against "banker mismanagement." Government has stolen and hoarded private gold stocks, has cheated creditors and money holders with an intentional policy of chronic inflation, has covered up bad banking with deceptive "regulatory accounting"—and yet bankers are deemed fraudulent and dishonest. With every mismanagement and deception conducted by central banking, and every instability it promotes, its favorable reputation only seems to grow, not diminish, while its power to inflict still further damage is extended, not constrained.

VI. Summary

Throughout U.S. history, bankers generally have been made scapegoats for banking crises that were essentially government created. Conventional explanations failed to correctly identify the true cause of these crises, and as a result, government intervention in money and banking grew considerably. Because the U.S. government has intervened in money and banking to enhance its own power, it has worked actively to blame the banking community for the detrimental effects of its interventions, in order to preserve its monetary privileges. Underlying this tragic pattern is the mistaken view that free banking is inherently unstable, while central banking promotes safe and sound banking. Interpretations of today's banking crisis continue the pattern. Only when this pattern is broken, when the damaging influence of central banking is fully recognized and fundamental reforms in favor of free banking and a gold standard are enacted, will future crises in the U.S. money and banking system be prevented.

Notes

1. Examples include Mayer (1990) and Pizzo, Fricker, and Muolo (1989). This theme of banker culpability has been applied equally to the S&L crisis, the banking crisis, and of course to problems on Wall Street.

2. See White (1989a; 1989b), Selgin (1988a), and Salsman (1990). "Free banking" means an unregulated system of money and credit, including the competitive issuance by private banks of currency convertible into some widely-accepted outside money, such as the precious metals. The system operates in the absence of a central bank and of any legal restrictions on bank operations; banks are subject only to the contract law and general bankruptcy law that apply to other industries.
3. Rockoff (1975; 1991) has demonstrated that wildcat banking was promoted by states that required privately issued bank notes to be collateralized by state bonds valued at par. This requirement was imposed primarily to ensure a source of financing for states. When the market value of the bonds fell below par value, there was an encouragement for bankers to over-issue notes and engage in fraud.
4. White (1983) and Smith (1936, 146–166) have shown that the inelastic currency of the post-Civil war period was due primarily to regulations requiring that private banknotes be collateralized by securities of the Federal government. These regulations impaired flexibility by making it difficult for banks to accommodate increases in the demand for currency relative to checking deposits. This problem is discussed more fully below.
5. Rothbard (1975) has shown that the inflation of the money supply by the Federal Reserve in the 1920s made the speculative boom possible and the resulting bust necessary. Friedman and Schwartz (1963, chapter 7) have shown that the Federal Reserve prolonged the banking crisis and the Great Depression by its inept management of the discount window and open-market operations. Phillips, McManus, and Nelson (1937) say the crisis of the 1930s was made possible exclusively by Federal Reserve mismanagement.
6. Other banks continued to operate as state-chartered institutions.
7. For a detailed discussion of each episode, see Sprague (1910).
8. Tallman (1988) makes this point. Calomiris and Gorton (1991, 114) show that the worst loss per deposit dollar during this era was only 2.1 cents, and the worst experience with bank failure rates was only 1.28%, in the Panic of 1893.
9. Chari (1989) demonstrates that these institutionally-imposed reserve pyramids made the U.S. banking system prone to panics, whereas Canada and Britain avoided both pyramids and panics.
10. Excerpts of the Comptroller's report are provided in Sprague (1910, 336).
11. Excerpts of the Treasury's report are provided in Sprague (1910, 330–31).
12. While their enthusiasm for this currency reform is understandable, Aldrich-Vreeland still did not permit banks full branching powers, unrestricted note issue, or unregulated reserves. On the other hand, to

the extent that the 1930s deflationary crisis was the inevitable result of the Federal Reserve's inflationary policies in the 1920s—a position endorsed by Phillips, McManus, and Nelson (1937) and Rothbard (1975), but not by Friedman and Schwartz—then in the Fed's "absence" the private banking system would never have faced the crisis of the early 1930s.

13. Cleveland and Huertas (1985, 59–61) describe the role of the National City Bank.
14. The procedure, referred to as "sterilizing" gold flows, was undertaken repeatedly in the 1920s, as described by Friedman and Schwartz (1963, 279–87), and was justified both as a means of "insulating" the U.S. from foreign economic influences, and of "assisting" Great Britain's return to the gold standard. According to the authors, "it probably would have been better . . . to have permitted the gold-standard rules to operate fully."
15. For evidence on the Fed inflating and encouraging speculation in the 1920s, see Rothbard (1975, chapter 5); for evidence on the Fed falling to meet the growing demand for currency, see Selgin (1988a, 638) as well as Friedman and Schwartz (1963, chapter 7). The sharp increase in the demand for currency, a demand that could not be met legally by banks and would not be supplied voluntarily by the Fed, is signified by the fall in the deposit-currency ratio from nearly twelve times in 1929 to less than five times in early 1933 (see Friedman and Schwartz 1963, 333). In turn, this falling ratio precipitated a collapse in the stock of money.
16. For example, in hearings held on the mix of commercial and investment banking, Senator Glass and others argued for a separation by defending the real bills doctrine, but made frequent references to the Pujo report to strengthen the case. See Kelly (1985, 48, 51–53).
17. During the depression, the National City Bank's capital ratio increased from 12% in 1929 to 15% in 1932, while the ratio of its brokerage affiliate rose from 62% to 70% over the same period. Unlike other banks, National City had also strengthened its liquidity to face the crises (Cleveland and Huertas 1985, 160–61, 169).
18. On the role of Willis, see Flannery (1985, 85, note 12); on the role of Glass, see Kelly (1985, 45).
19. See Kelly (1985, 43) and Flannery (1985, 67–69). Also, Friedman and Schwartz (1963, 244–45) point out that loans on securities were 38% of total bank loans in 1929, but had been only 3% in 1914.
20. See Kelly (1985, 52–53 and notes 148 and 152), who contends that Chase and National City were also motivated to weaken the competitive position of the rival Morgan bank. The Chairman of Chase National Bank, Winthrop Aldrich, actually assisted Senator Glass in drafting the legislation (Kelly 1985, 3, note 157).

21. See Chernow (1990, 357–59). This was the same Morgan Bank that in 1895 had defended the gold standard so courageously that it bailed out the U.S. Treasury with a $65 million gold loan, permitting the federal government to avoid suspending specie payments (Friedman and Schwartz, 1963, 111, note 35).
22. Gold coin and gold certificate confiscation was accomplished under the Emergency Banking Act signed into law by President Roosevelt on March 9, 1933 and included the power to declare the infamous "bank holiday." Gold clauses were abrogated under a separate act passed in 1933.
23. In October 1979 the Fed did concede the need to control the money supply and contain inflation, but by August 1982, when Mexico defaulted on its dollar-denominated debts, the Fed had again abandoned concern for inflation.
24. This was the contradictory and ill-named "Depository Institutions Deregulation and Monetary Control Act" of 1980. The "deregulation" was of deposit interest rates, over time. The "control" included the membership mandate, changes in reserve requirements, and extensions of FDIC coverage.
25. The "Financial Institutions Reform, Recovery, and Enforcement Act" of 1989 not only provided for a $50 billion taxpayer bailout (only one-tenth of the long-term expected cost of the S&L crisis) but granted significant interventionist powers to the Federal Deposit Insurance Corporation to regulate and seize banks with complete discretion. More recently, Congress has said it will replenish the bank deposit insurance fund *before* it grants banks "wider powers."
26. A study released in June 1991 by the Banking Committee in the U.S. House of Representatives found that 530 of the 2,990 banks that drew from the Fed's discount window between January 1985 and May 1991 failed within three years and that the Fed routinely lends to banks with the lowest possible rating that can be given by bank regulators. According to the report, Fed lending has allowed uninsured depositors to withdraw funds before banks are closed, shifting losses to the FDIC.
27. The bulk of the Fed's assets consist of interest-bearing government securities, while its liabilities primarily consist of non-interest-bearing Federal Reserve Notes (the country's monopoly currency) and non-interest-bearing deposits that count as reserves for member banks. The balance sheet alone explains the considerable profit margins the Fed generates. The Fed transfers most of its annual profit to the treasury, further evidence that the interests of government take precedence over those of the private banking system.
28. *Bank Failure: An Evaluation of the Factors Contributing to the Failure of the National Banks*, Office of the Comptroller of the Currency, Washington, D.C., 1988. This report continues a long tradition of similar

studies issued by the OCC over the years, all of which carefully evade the question of whether fraud has caused *systemic* instability (see Benston et al., 1986, 2–4).

29. "Banking-Fraud Convictions Nearly Double," *American Banker*, 1 August 1991.
30. See Lowell Bryan's "Banks Need Caps on Loans, Rates," *American Banker*, 19 June 1991, 4. New York Representative Charles Schumer, a member of the House Banking Committee, introduced legislation reflecting Bryan's plan during the summer of 1991.

References

Andrew, A. Piatt. "Substitutes for Cash in the Panic of 1907." *Quarterly Journal of Economics* (August 1908).

Benston, George J., et al. *Perspectives on Safe and Sound Banking: Past, Present, and Future*. Cambridge: MIT Press, 1986.

Calomiris, Charles W., and Gary Gorton. "The Origins of Banking Panics: Models, Facts, and Bank Regulation." In *Financial Markets and Financial Crises*, edited by R. Glenn Hubbard. Chicago: University of Chicago Press, 1991.

Chari, V. V. "Banking without Deposit Insurance or Bank Panics: Lessons from a Model of the U.S. National Banking System." *Quarterly Review* (1989). Federal Reserve Bank of Minneapolis.

Chernow, Ron. *The House of Morgan: An American Dynasty and the Rise of Modern Finance*. New York: Atlantic Monthly Press, 1990.

Cleveland, Harold van B., and Thomas F. Huertas. *Citibank, 1812–1970*. Cambridge: Harvard University Press, 1985.

Flannery, Mark J. "An Economic Evaluation of Bank Securities Activities Before 1933." In *Deregulating Wall Street: Commercial Bank Penetration of the Corporate Securities Market*, edited by Ingo Walter. New York: Wiley, 1985.

Friedman, Milton, and Anna J. Schwartz. *A Monetary History of the United States, 1867–1960*. Princeton: Princeton University Press, 1963.

Glasner, David. *Free Banking and Monetary Reform*. New York: Cambridge University Press, 1989.

Goodhart, Charles. *The Evolution of Central Banks*. Cambridge: MIT Press, 1988.

Gorton, Gary. "Private Clearinghouses and the Origins of Central Banking." *Business Review* (1984). Federal Reserve Bank of Philadelphia.

———. "Bank Suspensions of Convertibility." *Journal of Monetary Economics* (March 1985): 177–93.

Groseclose, Elgin. *America's Money Machine: The Story of the Federal Reserve*. Westport, Conn.: Arlington House, 1980.

Horwitz, Steven. "Competitive Currencies, Legal Restrictions, and the Origins of the Fed: Some Evidence from the Panic of 1907." *Southern Economic Journal* (1990).

Kelly, Edward J. "Legislative History of the Glasis-Steagall Act." In *Deregulating Wall Street: Commercial Bank Penetration of the Corporate Securities Market,* edited by Ingo Walter. New York, Wiley, 1985.

Mayer, Martin. *The Greatest-Ever Bank Robbery: The Collapse of the Savings and Loan Industry.* New York: Macmillan, 1990.

Noyes, Alexander Dana. *Thirty Years of American Finance: A Short Financial History of the Government and People of the United States Since the Civil War, 1865–1896.* New York: Putnam, 1910.

Office of the Comptroller of the Currency. *Bank Failure: An Evaluation of the Factors Contributing to the Failure of National Banks.* Washington, D.C., 1988.

Pecora, Ferdinand. *Wall Street Under Oath: The Story of Our Modern Money Changers.* New York: Simon and Schuster, 1939.

Phillips, C. A., T. F. McManus, and R. W. Nelson. *Banking and the Business Cycle: A Study of the Great Depression in the United States.* New York: Macmillan, 1937.

Pizzo, Stephen, Mary Fricker, and Paul Muolo. *Inside Job: The Looting of America's Savings and Loans.* New York: McGraw-Hill, 1989.

Rockoff, Hugh. *The Free Banking Era: A Re-examination.* New York: Arno, 1975.

———. "Lessons from the American Experience with Free Banking." In *Unregulated Banking: Chaos or Order?,* edited by Forrest Capie and Geoffrey E. Wood. New York: St. Martin's, 1991.

Roosevelt, Franklin D. *The Public Papers of Franklin D. Roosevelt.* New York: Random House, 1938.

Rothbard, Murray. *America's Great Depression.* Kansas City, Mo.: Sheed and Ward, 1975.

Salsman, Richard M. *Breaking the Banks: Central Banking Problems and Free Banking Solutions.* Great Barrington, Mass.: American Institute for Economic Research, 1990.

Schwartz, Anna J. "Real and Pseudo-Financial Crises." *Financial Crises and the World Banking System,* edited by Forrest Capie and Geoffrey E. Wood. New York: St. Martin's, 1986.

Selgin, George A. *The Theory of Free Banking: Money Supply Under Competitive Note Issue.* Totowa, N.J.: Rowman and Littlefield, 1988a.

———. "Accomodating Changes in the Relative Demand for Currency: Free Banking vs. Central Banking." *Cato Journal* 7 (1988b): 621–41.

Shughart, William F., II. "A Public Choice Perspective of the Banking Act of 1933," *Cato Journal* 7 (1988): 595–613.

Smith, Vera C. *The Rationale of Central Banking and the Free Banking Alternative.* Indianapolis: Liberty Press, 1990. Orig. pub. 1936.

Sobel, Robert. *Panic on Wall Street: A History of America's Financial Disasters.* New York: Macmillan, 1968.

Sprague, O. M. W. *History of Crises Under the National Banking System.* Washington, D.C.: Government Printing Office, 1910. Study sponsored by the National Monetary Commission.

Tallman, Ellis. "Some Unanswered Questions about Bank Panics." *Economic Review* (December 1988). Federal Reserve Bank of Atlanta. December 1988.

Timberlake, Richard H. *The Origins of Central Banking in the United States.* Cambridge: Harvard University Press, 1978.

———. "The Central Banking Role of Clearinghouse Associations." *Journal of Money, Credit, and Banking* (February 1984).

———. "Seventy-Five Years of Monetary Control." *Durell Journal of Money and Banking.* (November 1989): 2–9, 30–38.

White, Eugene N. *The Regulation and Reform of the American Banking System, 1900–1929.* Princeton: Princeton University Press, 1983.

———. "Before the Glass-Steagall Act: An Analysis of the Investment Banking Activities of National Banks." *Explorations in Economic History* (1986): 33–55.

White, Lawrence H. *Competition and Currency: Essays on Free Banking and Money.* New York: New York University Press, 1989a.

———. "The Growing Scarcity of Banknotes in the United States, 1865–1913." Unpublished manuscript, University of Georgia, 1989b.

5

Deposit Insurance Reform Is Not Enough

Walker Todd and Gerald P. O'Driscoll, Jr.

Deposit insurance reform is the cornerstone of virtually every banking reform proposal. The deficiencies of the present system of deposit insurance are widely acknowledged, and debate has turned increasingly to how, and not whether, the system should be changed.[1]

In this chapter we argue that deposit insurance reform alone cannot solve the structural instabilities of the U.S. banking system. Deposit insurance is only one part of the federal financial safety net that undergirds the banking industry. Other elements of the safety net reinforce and enhance the perverse incentives generated by deposit insurance. Hence, policymakers cannot expect to achieve a more stable banking system by limiting themselves to even comprehensive deposit insurance reform.[2] Further, we cite the reasons why any form of deposit insurance will prevent the United States from achieving a stable and equitable banking system.

In the section that follows, we trace the evolution of the U.S. banking system and the seemingly innocuous incorporation of deposit guarantees by both the state and federal governments. The analysis includes an examination of early problems with deposit insurance, using the Kansas experience as a representative case. We then review the inadequacies of current reform proposals and the prospects for more comprehensive reform, the reform of deposit insurance. In our conclusion, we suggest a number of market mechanisms for achieving genuine reform of the banking system.

I. From Regulation to Ownership: The Evolution of U.S. Banking Regulation

Banking, in at least some of its forms, has always been regulated in the United States. From time to time, however, government has subjected aspects of banking to greater or lesser scrutiny. For instance, historians describe banking from 1838 to 1863 as the era of "free banking." The freedom they refer to, however, was limited to the acquisition of bank charters: prior to the period, each new bank charter required a special and specific legislative act. The system provided ample opportunity for bribery and subtler forms of corruption of legislatures. Free banking allowed those desiring to incorporate a bank to meet only certain specified and general legal tests, such as minimum capital requirements, in order to obtain a charter. The change diminished the potential for political corruption in the chartering process. It also enhanced competition. What was "free" in the free-banking era was entry.

Banks were never empowered freely to enter new activities or, until comparatively recently and only in some states, to branch freely into new geographical markets. Public law and policy have always placed significant limitations on bank powers and branching rights. Banks in the United States have never had anything like the commercial freedom accorded to most other enterprises. Indeed, the evolution of legal and political doctrine has denied banks even basic privileges and immunities accorded to individuals and other kinds of corporations.[3] The rationale for these restrictions has always been that banking is "clothed in the public interest."

Regardless, the government's relation to banking has changed dramatically in the short history of our country. A series of incremental legal and policy changes has wrought a major revolution in the relationship between the government, especially the federal government, and the banking industry. Put starkly but accurately, the outcome of this revolution was the substantial nationalization of the U.S. banking industry (Kane 1985, 23). What makes this nationalization especially perverse, however, is that the government underwrites most of the banking system's liabilities without taking legal title to the capital or the assets.

Before the Civil War, the states tended to be sovereign in all matters save those specifically reserved for the federal government.[4] Chartering corporations was a power shared between the states and the federal government. In the antebellum period, however, only two corporations, the First and Second Banks of the United States, received federal charters. Save for these two important episodes in U.S. history, the federal government left bank chartering exclusively and bank regulation largely to the states.

The involvement of the state governments in banking was pervasive. The states often regulated banks in great detail and intervened in bank operations occasionally, as when they sanctioned the suspension of specie payment during the numerous banking crises of the nineteenth century. In the antebellum United States, however, save in the aftermath of the panic of 1837, state governments avoided underwriting banking or bailing banks out of financial difficulties. In this limited sense, banking fit a laissez faire model. If entry was not always free, exit through failure was largely unregulated.

The National Bank Act of 1863 represented the first significant intrusion by the federal government into banking regulation. It also marked the first instance in which the federal government underwrote any aspect of banking.[5] Among other things, the act authorized the chartering of national banks and the issuance of a new currency—national bank notes. The act required national banks to deposit federal government bonds with the Treasury equal in value to 111% of the face value of the notes. (The amount was later reduced to 100% and further amended.) As Friedman and Schwartz (1963, 21) observed, "Though national bank notes were nominally liabilities of the banks that issued them, in effect they were indirect liabilities of the federal government." Upon failure of a national bank, the Treasury was authorized to redeem all the bank's notes in circulation, and the bonds securing the notes were then forfeited to the U.S. government.

Although literally true, the assertion that the federal government stood behind the issuance of national bank notes is potentially misleading in the modern context of debates on the wisdom and propriety of federal deposit insurance. In the event of an insolvency, the government used the bank's own assets to redeem the notes. National bank failures ordinarily could not trigger a taxpayer bailout. Indeed, the taxpayer was insulated from liability several times over. For instance, other provisions of the act gave the Treasury first lien on all assets of a failed bank and upon the personal liability of the bank's stockholders to cover any shortfalls between the par value of the notes and the face value of the bonds. Further, after 1874, there was a redemption fund kept on deposit with the Treasury (Friedman and Schwartz 1963, 20–21).

The contrast between nineteenth-century banking policy and current federal banking policy could scarcely be greater. Under the National Bank Act, only a certain class of the liabilities of national banks was guaranteed. The amount of the bank's eligible bonds pledged strictly limited the aggregate amount of bank liabilities covered by the federal government. Government fiscal policy could change the theoretical maximum of the guaranteed national bank liabilities, but privately acting bankers could not (Friedman and Schwartz 1963, 23).[6] Hence, taxpayer liability was virtually nonexistent. If the National Bank Act was a foot in the door to later approval of a blanket government guarantee of bank liabilities, it was a very tentative and unintrusive entry that no one involved contemplated at the time.

Today, the federal government places few limitations on the size and type of liabilities it will guarantee for the banking system. Contemporary taxpayers have been made fully liable for nearly the entire amount of the guarantees. The taxpayer's liability is potential and indirect only so long as the deposit insurance fund has adequate resources. Now that liability is becoming real as fund resources disappear. Worse, not only is the potential taxpayer liability for bank failures immense, but the actions of politically unaccountable private individuals (bankers)—not elected representatives—determine the amount and timing of the draw on the taxpayer. One can hardly construct a less market-oriented or more inequitable system.

Experimentation with Deposit Insurance: The Kansas Experience

The transformation of nineteenth century banking policy into that of the present involved a number of steps. The common denominator of the change, however, was the implementation of governmentally sponsored deposit guarantees. In response to the financial panic of 1907, eight states established some form of deposit guarantee system between 1907 and 1917.[7] Membership by state banks was compulsory in some of those states and voluntary in others. All eight systems failed, some more quickly than others. The state of Washington's system ended the most ignominiously: "Washington's system was the shortest-lived. In 1921, following the state's first bank failure, which happened also to be the largest insured bank, all other banks withdrew from the system." (Wheelock and Kumbhakar 1990, 10). This was adverse selection with a vengeance.

Studies of the Kansas system by Wheelock and Kumbhakar reveal that in some ways it was the most promising of the state systems. Like Washington, the Kansas system called for voluntary participation by the state's banks. Although this characteristic was a drawback in the Washington case, Kansas regulators made a virtue out of necessity. Opponents of deposit insurance had argued that it penalized conservative banks by compelling them to fund the costs of failed institutions. To mollify this opposition, the Kansas law limited coverage to demand deposits not paying interest and to certain savings accounts with interest rates limited to 3%. More important, the law established strict capital requirements and required banks to be inspected before receiving coverage (Wheelock and Kumbhakar 1990, 6–7). It is instructive to compare these restrictions with today's deposit insurance system, which covers high yielding, brokered deposits in banks with little or no capitalization.

Wheelock and Kumbhakar (8) describe the Kansas' fund's supervision of its insured banks as "relatively strict," and the system in fact achieved a degree of success for several years. "Between 1909 and 1919 there were just eight failures of state chartered banks in Kansas, and only two of them had been members of the insurance system" (Wheelock and Kumbhakar 1990, 9). The system's success, however, rapidly deteriorated once agricultural distress struck the state in the early 1920s. Bank losses skyrocketed and regulators were forced to impose special assessments on insured banks. Predictably, banks began to flee the system, and by 1926 it was hopelessly insolvent.[8]

One might suppose that economic conditions were responsible for the wave of Kansas bank failures in the 1920s (just as some blame falling energy prices for the recent banking debacle in Texas). If the supposition were accurate, then the state deposit insurance system would be exonerated from responsibility. The facts are inconsistent, however, with this view. Consider the following table, constructed from information in Wheelock and Kumbhakar (9).

Kansas Bank Failures, 1920–26

Period	*Insured*	*Uninsured*
1920–22	17 (2.5%)	6 (1.4%)
1922–24	42 (5.9%)	12 (3.0%)
1924–26	35 (5.3%)	10 (2.6%)

The percentages in parentheses indicate the proportion of banks in that category that failed in the indicated two-year period. More telling than the evident difference between failure rates among insured and uninsured state banks was the experience of national banks in the same time period: "There were no failures of national banks in the first two-year period, four from 1922–24 (1.5% of national banks), and two from 1924–26 (0.8% of national banks)" (Wheelock and Kumbhakar 1990, 9).

If economic conditions were not responsible for the rash of Kansas bank failures, what made the state's deposit insurance system accountable for those failures? Did insurance coverage lead banks to become riskier—the moral hazard problem—or did risky banks apply for insurance in disproportionate numbers—the adverse selection dilemma? The econometric problems inherent in determining the importance of each factor are difficult to resolve.

Regardless of which effect dominated, the Kansas experience pointed (and points) to the pitfalls of government guarantees of deposits. Even though the Kansas system had safeguards to prevent both moral hazard and adverse selection, the system did not avoid an abnormally high failure rate of insured banks. The high failure rate existed despite the state's enforcement of these risk-taking controls. Further, the system was voluntary, as would be a private insurance or reinsurance system. Indeed, the Kansas experience raises questions about the ability of insurers to gauge financial risk in banking, or even to sort out good banks from bad.

Moving Toward the Nationalization of U.S. Banking

During the same time that states were experimenting with guarantee systems, the federal government was conducting an experiment of its own. The Federal Reserve System, created in 1913, promised a degree of security for national banks and member state banks. The new bankers' bank was designed in part to provide a means to liquify previously illiquid assets. The device created to provide liquidity was the discount window. At the discount window, member commercial banks could deposit short-term, commercial loans to act as collateral against advances of ready cash. The system was not a direct guarantee of deposits but could operate indirectly in a similar fashion. During a financial crisis or local economic downturn (such as occurred periodically in agricultural regions), good assets could be converted into cash temporarily. No longer did banks need to dump illiquid assets at fire-sale prices to raise cash with which to pay off depositors.

Although not a deposit guarantee, the discount window was a potential source of problems if regulators used the device for more than transitory banking difficulties. For a number of years, however, central bank doctrine, as enunciated by Walter Bagehot in the 1870s, prevented abuse of the discount window by recommending that the central banks lend only to solvent banks and only against good collateral. Supporters of Bagehot's lender of last resort concept contended that the central bank was not intended or designed to keep insolvent banks open. Moreover, bank closure rules, including criminal penalties for bank officers and directors who continued to receive deposits while knowing that their bank was insolvent, operated to prevent bailing out insolvent banks through the discount window. The loss experience during the onset of the Great Depression suggests that bank regulators performed their duty remarkably well even under the most difficult circumstances. From 1930 to 1933, average annual losses incurred by depositors in bank failures before the advent of federal deposit insurance were .81% of total deposits (Benston 1986, 64).

In the last few years, classical central bank doctrine has been honored more in the breach than in practice. Bank regulators routinely keep insolvent banks open, often by using discount window lending to substitute for private liabilities. In so doing, regulators confound protection of the banking *system* with protection of individual institutions. The contemporary course of action runs directly contrary to classical central bank doctrine.

When an insolvent commercial bank is eventually disposed of under current policy, the Federal Reserve Banks' loans are repaid by the Bank Insurance Fund (BIF). This draws down BIF's reserves, which derive from premium assessments on commercial banks. At some point—now reached if not breached—BIF itself becomes insolvent. Taxpayers' funds will then be drawn upon. Thus, violating classical principles of central banking converts unsound banking policy into unsound fiscal policy. The current policy is fiscally important because it affects the size of the federal budget deficit. It is unsound in law and in political economy because the fiscal effects are the product not of deliberate congressional actions but of the actions of private agents (bankers) and unelected decision makers at federal agencies.

Prior to the Federal Reserve Act, national banks were subject to both regulatory and market disciplines. Although the comptroller of the currency examined the banks regularly, private clearing houses monitored banks on a day-to-day basis. Clearinghouses could quickly detect telltale signs of unsafe and unsound banking. Because their membership was directly exposed to the consequences, it was often the clearinghouse that imposed discipline on shaky banks (White 1989, 230–33).

With the creation of the Federal Reserve System, reserve banks assumed many of the roles of the clearinghouses, eliminating some of the market control. With the loss of these market controls, the need for governmental supervision and regulation became greater. In 1933, Congress created another agency, the Federal Deposit Insurance Corporation (FDIC), to help monitor banks. The creation of the Federal Savings and Loan Insurance Corporation followed in 1935 for savings and loan associations.

The ostensible purpose of the FDIC was to protect the small depositor. The idea was that small depositors were unable to distinguish sound from unsound banks. Massive bank failures, such as occurred in the 1930s, led small depositors to withdraw their funds from the banking system. That is, the bank failures had led to a contagious run on sound banks, conversion of deposits into currency, and the concomitant shrinkage of the money supply and economic disruption. A system of federal deposit insurance, the government surmised, would restore confidence and stability in the banking system.

In the beginning, the FDIC operated in a manner broadly consistent with its stated purpose. Insurance was initially established at $2,500 per account. Over the years, however, the ceiling has been raised successively. The most recent, famous, and fateful change was in 1980, when the ceiling went up to $100,000. To put the issue in perspective, if coverage had been kept constant in real terms, it should be approximately $20,000 today. Worse, under the doctrine of "too big to fail," deposits at large banks are protected no matter their amount. The cumulative effect of these policies has left the FDIC facing insolvency.

In less than sixty years, we have come full circle. We have a troubled banking system and insufficient resources to resolve future failures. The legacy of sixty years of deposit insurance is twofold: subsidized lending to excessively risky projects, most visible today in commercial real estate; and the so-called credit crunch, the starvation of the productive element of the economy for resources due to the previous overcommitment to risky projects.

Because the disastrous effects of federal deposit insurance are so conspicuous, it is hardly surprising that so much attention is focused on deposit insurance reform. Unfortunately, other aspects of banking have changed as well. Bank supervision is more relaxed, and policy allows banks to take greater risks. As a result, were deposit insurance eliminated tomorrow, these other changes would probably generate much the same moral hazard problem that we have today. The temptation we must avoid, then, is to take a piecemeal approach to overall banking reform, concentrating fundamental reform efforts on deposit insurance alone. Sadly, as the following section demonstrates, the sentiment for piecemeal reform is pervasive.

II. Avoiding Fundamental Reform: The Latest Banking Band-Aids

As the evidence suggesting that the BIF is approaching not merely illiquidity but actual insolvency continues to mount, the debate about banking reform has begun to take some unpredicted and, probably, unpredictable turns. For example, in mid-March 1991, the Treasury announced a recapitalization plan for the BIF. The plan proposed that the FDIC use an undrawn $5 billion credit line with the Treasury as the equivalent of equity or net worth to support FDIC borrowings in the public debt market. The borrowing would be made through the Federal Financing Bank (FFB), which coordinates Treasury and government agency borrowings in the market.

The authorization for such FDIC public debt borrowing came from the Financial Institutions Reform, Recovery, and Enforcement Act of 1989 (FIRREA). FIRREA enables the FDIC to borrow on a 9-to-1 leveraging ratio against its net worth. The act also increased the FDIC's Treasury credit line from $3 billion to the present $5 billion.

Because the FDIC's net worth already is at or below zero on a market-value basis, the FDIC wishes to count the Treasury credit line as equity against which it can borrow up to $45 billion through the FFB. If the FDIC does so, its available Treasury credit line would be reduced gradually to zero as the full $45 billion were borrowed. The FDIC apparently expected to use the $45 billion for what it terms "working capital" for BIF. "Working capital" constitutes the funding required to carry assets assumed from failed or failing banks on the BIF's books pending the resale or other liquidation of those assets.

Unfortunately, even this $45 billion would not solve the financial problems of the FDIC. One might assume, quite realistically, that the remaining $4 billion in the BIF at year-end 1990 would cover only the 150 to 200 small-bank failures that recent history suggests will take place through 1991. If, however, the FDIC were to move aggressively to resolve some of the larger, lingering bank failures and open-but-failing bank problems, even more funds would be required.[9]

The FDIC apparently has contemplated the potential shortfall it would face were it to recognize the additional BIF losses that acquisition of the assets of these other failed and failing banks would generate. The agency formally asked Congress for permission to borrow up to $25 billion directly from "any Federal Reserve Bank," *in addition* to the $45 billion of working capital borrowings described above (Title IV of the Treasury's draft banking reform bill). Although press reports indicated that the FDIC wanted to repay the Fed borrowings over fifteen years, the draft bill specified no maturity. Further, the FDIC proposed to repay the Fed by increasing the premium rate for deposit insurance from twenty-three basis points (.23%) per annum to thirty basis points—an amount that would begin to approach one-half of the total earnings of a typical New York money center bank in any recent good year.

As late as mid-March 1991, the Federal Reserve Board was tacitly supporting the FDIC's borrowing request. The board even went so far as to circulate internal staff memoranda to the effect that the emergency lending provisions of the Federal Reserve Act already authorized the Fed to make such loans to the FDIC. About one week later, the staff of the U.S. Senate Banking Committee was induced to arrive at a similar conclusion.

Despite the board's support for an FDIC bailout loan, however, literature squarely contradicting the board's position on the subject already existed in the public domain (Todd 1988, appendix A; Hackley 1973, esp. 195–201). Toward the end of March, press reports indicated that the regional reserve bank presidents were expressing objections to the board's position on a bailout loan for the FDIC.

Compare this reaction with the reaction of the same parties two years earlier, when a comparable bailout scheme for the former Federal Savings and Loan Insurance Corporation (FSLIC), the "Joint

Lending Program," was presented to the reserve banks. At that time, no one objected in the presence of the governors or presidents, and only two reserve banks delayed their formal acquiescence to the scheme by one additional business day. The Federal Home Loan Bank of San Francisco held back its acceptance of the plan for two weeks, but the other home loan banks acquiesced about as quickly as the reserve banks.

Two years later, the lessons learned by the Federal Reserve System with respect to the funding of other agencies of the government enabled Chairman Alan Greenspan to articulate a well-grounded theoretical case against the FDIC bailout loan request in his testimony before the Senate Banking Committee on April 23, 1991. Chairman Greenspan noted, correctly, that Congress has always severely limited and, more recently, has allowed to expire statutes authorizing the direct placement of Treasury debt with the Federal Reserve. This long-standing policy apparently reflects concern of monetary, as distinguished from fiscal, authorities that such a practice could compromise the independent conduct of monetary policy and would allow the Treasury to escape the discipline of selling its debt directly to the market. Implementation of the Treasury funding proposal could have created perceptions, both in the United States and abroad, that the nature or function of our central bank had been altered. In addition, if implementation of the proposal created a precedent for further loans to BIF or to other entities, the liquidity of the Federal Reserve's portfolio could have been reduced sufficiently over time to create concerns about the ability of the Federal Reserve to control the supply of reserves and, thereby, to achieve its monetary policy objectives (Greenspan 1991, 18). The *New York Times* reported that Chairman Greenspan told the Banking Committee that the central bank did not see itself as a lender of last resort for the bank fund (BIF). There is "no sound economic reason" to use the Fed instead of the Treasury for that purpose, he said (Hershey 1991).

Nevertheless, the Treasury still resists learning this necessary and useful lesson.[10] The real problem, however, may be that the Treasury insufficiently understands the monetary and fiscal consequences of the distinction between, on the one hand, central bank loans to member banks on good collateral for liquidity purposes and, on the other hand, fifteen-year unsecured loans of capital to a government agency (Todd 1988). That distinction is what separates liquidity concerns from capital (insolvency) problems; failure to observe the distinction tends to convert fiscal problems into monetary problems.

III. Practical Objections to the Current Deposit Insurance System

Essentially, the existing federal deposit insurance system, like the Kansas system of the 1920s and the earlier state safety or insurance funds, has caused the least well-capitalized, riskiest institutions to rely increasingly on deposit insurance to raise funds at costs (yields) well below those that depositors would demand in the absence of federal deposit insurance. The larger institutions rely more heavily on cheap, insured deposit funds in absolute dollar amounts than do similarly situated, smaller institutions, even though the smaller institutions rely more heavily on deposit insurance as a proportion of all deposit accounts.[11] Thus, when enough of the larger institutions begin to fail, the drain on the deposit insurance funds will be larger, in absolute dollar amounts, and will overwhelm the remaining or realistically potential resources of the BIF. The BIF's shortfall will give rise to calls for taxpayer-funded bailouts, central bank-funded bailout loans, and the like. This problematic scenario is inevitable and incurable in a politically sensitive bank supervisory structure that cannot and will not rein in the risk-taking activities of the largest insured institutions until it is too late.

In contrast, the classic, pre-1933 approach to bank failure resolution offers the following virtues:

1. Large depositors and other claimants would be forced to share losses pro rata.
2. Managers and shareholders would be subject to some type of direct, personal liability for shortfalls between banks' asset and liability values, which would make them more prudent in their lending and investment decisions. (In the case of stockholders, there formerly was supplemental liability equal to their original investment.)
3. Uninsured depositors typically would recover close to the full value of their deposits, over time.
4. Taxpayers and the central bank ordinarily would be spared the cost of underwriting payoffs of large depositors. In an environment in which the arithmetic mean insured deposit account is about $10,000, it is either a reverse transfer program, or a subsidy of the few by the many, to tax average depositors to pay off

> $100,000 deposits. The average depositor, at least, ordinarily would be better off if everyone were left alone to bear his or her own losses.

Aside from the practical difficulties cited above, the principal problem that deposit insurance poses for economists is that it is inconsistent with a well-functioning market system. Hence, any discussion of deposit insurance reform necessarily descends into a third- and fourth-order analysis of problems.

It is essential to keep the derivation of modern U.S. banking structure in mind when reviewing deposit insurance reform proposals. In a state of nature, when people come to agree on a conventional standard of value that they call "money," it is inevitable that some will have more and others less of it at any given moment (Aristotle 1987, 160–63). Thus, some will lend money and others will borrow it. The lenders might be called "bankers," particularly when they borrow from others—or accept deposits of money—for the purpose of relending.

By the eighteenth century in England, some bankers sought the legal protection of corporate charters. Others did not and continued to engage in banking as individuals or in partnerships. It is difficult, then, to argue that a corporate charter is essential to banking, although it is undeniable that such a charter is convenient to some bankers. Some commercial bankers continue to operate as partnerships, without corporate charters. Banking in corporate form is only a second-order concern for market-oriented economists, yet one that (perhaps wrongly) today is almost taken for granted, as though incorporated commercial banking itself were part of the state of nature.

When we learned in the 1930s that even incorporated commercial bankers are capable of failure, the idea of federal deposit insurance was born. Banking reformers of the 1930s, many of whom were fond of central planning, recognized that all that deposit insurance could accomplish would be to make risk taking safer for bad bankers. The reformers allowed the creation of the FDIC and FSLIC, however, to gain congressional votes for other banking reform measures. Thus, insured-deposit, incorporated commercial banking (mortgage banking, in the case of savings and loans) was born. Such an activity should be of no greater than third-order concern because its principal underpinnings already are quite remote from the principles of a market economy.

The 1970s and early 1980s witnessed the inception of a new doctrine, "too big or too important to fail." Thus, the third-order concern described above became a fourth-order concern, unlimited insured-deposit, incorporated commercial banking.[12] This concept truly is so removed from a market economy, being corporatist and dirigiste in its origins, that it is a wonder the existing system has any support among economists. Yet proposals are still put forth for "market-oriented deposit insurance reform," as though "federal deposit insurance" logically belongs in the same sentence as "market oriented."

Other practical objections to some of the ideas currently being considered in pursuit of nominally market-oriented deposit insurance reform may be briefly stated:

1. A federally guaranteed program of deposit insurance to be administered, at the first level, by private-sector bankers probably is unconstitutional and definitely proves far more costly to taxpayers than any conceivable benefit that they might derive from it. Such a program probably is unconstitutional because Congress cannot delegate the power to create legally binding, full-faith-and-credit claims on the U.S. Treasury to private sector bankers who are unaccountable to the political process. Also, Congress already is aware that, without amending the Constitution, it cannot bind any future Congress to appropriate monies to repay deposit insurance guarantees of indefinite amount and duration that might be issued today. Thus, FIRREA specifies that only FDIC obligations having definite principal amounts and definite maturity dates have the full-faith-and-credit guarantee. Such obligations are constitutionally binding, but indefinite guarantees issued by the FDIC are not, and such concerns should be borne in mind as we debate market-oriented reforms of deposit insurance.
2. Any taxpayer benefit from federal deposit insurance is lost when the cost of keeping the program going exceeds the payout to insured depositors. To date, the present value cost of the FSLIC rescue, about $230 billion total, is nearly $2,000 per tax return, while the arithmetic mean FSLIC-insured account still is about $8,000. The cost/benefit tradeoff in the BIF might prove disadvantageous to the average depositor/taxpayer, however, because of the much greater proportion of uninsured deposits in the largest commercial banks. The eventual BIF rescue cost also could

reach $2,000 per tax return. With mean BIF-insured accounts in the range of $12,000, if enough "too big to fail" institutions are rescued, with large proportions of uninsured deposits, then, in those institutions, at least, it is foreseeable that the per-taxpayer cost would exceed the per-mean-depositor insured amounts.

3. Federal deposit insurance and other elements of the federal safety net for banking constitute a federal subsidy of commercial banking. For whom, exactly, is the subsidy intended? The current system favors bank managers and shareholders to the detriment of depositors in their role as taxpayers. Anyone can purchase highly liquid Treasury bills paying competitive yields in maturities as short as three months and in denominations as small as $10,000. Small savers can purchase savings bonds paying competitive yields that may be cashed in after only six months in denominations as small as $100. Hence, savers already have competitive-yield, default-free alternatives to insured-deposit, incorporated commercial banking.
4. Using central bank funds (either discount window advances or allocations of government securities purchases) either to liquify or guarantee the solvency of a federal deposit insurance fund is a dangerous use of monetary reserves or of the monetary base-creating mechanism. If not sterilized, such central bank activity would be inflationary.
5. Politically driven pressures on the deposit insurance fund and the central bank (the Federal Reserve) to bail out failing institutions will not subside as long as any level of federal deposit insurance exists. Assume, for argument's sake, that the insured deposit limit were reduced to $10,000 (the Treasury bill minimum denomination). If a large bank were in danger of failing with some insured but mostly uninsured deposits, however, the existing political realities still would exert enormous pressure on central bank and insurance fund bureaucrats to find a way to bail that bank out, including protection of the uninsured depositors. It is the very existence of deposit insurance at any level, or of a central bank discount window rationale that contemplates any solvency support lending at all (temporary or longer-term), that creates the apparently irresistible temptation for policymakers to meddle in the market-exit process for failing banks. None of this meddling, of course, has anything whatsoever to do with a market-oriented desire for competitive efficiency in commercial banking (Mayer 1991).

IV. Reform Proposals

It should come as no surprise that we recommend eliminating governmental provision of deposit insurance. Whether a system of private (competitive) deposit insurance might arise in its stead is problematical (O'Driscoll 1988). But, as we argued above, practical, political, and economic considerations argue against continuation of even a scaled-back federal deposit insurance system. Absent the abolition of federal deposit insurance, we offer some structural reforms that still would reduce the perverse incentives of the current federal financial safety net. We do not hide our ultimate goal and hope that these reforms would facilitate more substantial and far-reaching policy changes.

Outline of Reforms

A. Deposit Insurance
  1. Enforce insured deposit limits strictly.
  2. Reduce deposit insurance ceilings in semiannual stages of $10,000, until the upper limit is only $10,000. We choose this figure because it represents the minimum denomination of Treasury bills. The amount also corresponds roughly to the arithmetic mean of insured deposits.
  3. Retain liquidation operations of the FDIC, but merge the Resolution Trust Corporation (RTC) into the FDIC. Allow the RTC to disappear after the current 1996 statutory expiration date.
  4. Sharply limit the use of conservatorships and bridge banks to handle insolvent banks. The technique currently is used only because the FDIC has insufficient resources to close the insolvent institutions. With each conservatorship or bridge bank appointment, the FDIC should be required to submit a request to Congress for the needed funds.

B. Supervisory Reforms
  1. Rely primarily on market-value accounting statements in assessing solvency and capital adequacy.
  2. Publish and adhere to early intervention and early closure standards in order to reduce, if not eliminate, losses to the insurance fund and uninsured creditors.

C. Discount Window
Return to the classic central bank doctrine of lending only on good collateral to solvent institutions. Allow unsound banks to fail and be promptly closed.

Obviously, these proposals do not exhaust possible remedies. But even these few would go a long way toward needed reform. Moreover, the proposals are mutually supporting. For instance, if supervisors used market-value accounting and adhered to early closure rules, then the FDIC fund would be protected and the current use of conservatorships and bridge banks would become unnecessary. Over time, we predict, the now "politically impossible" reform of eliminating deposit insurance entirely would become viable. This would occur as the public, Congress, and the administration come to understand the magnitude of the gap between the costs of maintaining the current system, and the lower costs of the proposed reform system.

Notes

The views expressed in this chapter are those of the authors alone, and should not be attributed to the Federal Reserve Banks of Dallas or Cleveland, or to the Federal Reserve System.

1. As we write, the administration's banking reform proposal is in committee. Deposit insurance refunding is a central part of the proposal. Indeed, many feel that it may be the only part of the proposal with a significant chance of passage (Knight 1991).
2. Unless otherwise noted, in this chapter we use "banking" generically to cover all types of deposit-taking institutions.
3. See, for instance, Article IV, Sections 1 and 2 of the U.S. Constitution for an important set of privileges and immunities that statutory and case law have come to deny to banks.
4. More accurately, the states were sovereign in all matters governmental. This reflected their place in common law as the inheritors of the rights granted by the original crown grants creating each colony. Constitutionally, the Ninth Amendment is crucial in determining the respective locus of decision-making power among the people, the states, and the central government (Barnett 1989). Politically, the Civil War decisively shifted the locus of power to the central government and away from the states and the people.

5. The federal government did provide special treatment for the First and Second Banks of the United States. For example, the banks' notes were receivable for taxes and lawful money; other banks did not have this privilege.
6. National banks never issued anything like the theoretical maximum total. Only in the 1920s did the note issue reach 80% of its maximum permissible amount. In the nineteenth and early twentieth centuries, the circulation was closer to 20% of the maximum (Friedman and Schwartz 1963, 23). The shortfall remains a theoretical and historical conundrum.
7. The eight were Oklahoma, Texas, Kansas, Washington, Nebraska, South Dakota, North Dakota, and Mississippi (White 1983, 210–11).
8. Wheelock and Kumbhakar (10) quote the state bank commissioner's report for 1926: "In my view of the above I can see little to encourage one to believe that the guaranty fund will ever pay out, and it is my hope that the next legislature will repeal the law."
9. At this writing, the FDIC's bridge bank for the Bank of New England (about $20 billion of assets at book value) is being resolved through sale to a bidder (apparently, Fleet/Norstar and the Kohlberg, Kravis, Roberts investment partnership) at a net cost that the FDIC estimates at $2.5 billion. However, a realistic case can be made for the proposition that a net cost to the BIF closer to $3.3 billion would be more accurate. Other large bank holding companies (assets in excess of $10 billion each) whose principal bank subsidiaries may face failure in the near term (measured from market-to-book value ratios below 40% as of September 18, 1991, according to the *American Banker*) include companies with the following ratios: 7.6%, 30.4%, 33.7%, 34.1%, and 35.0%, only one of which is in New England. The common shares of these institutions are traded in the $2 to $3 price range. In addition, the shares of a few other larger institutions barely surpassed the 40% threshold, even at the peak of the recent run-up in banks' share prices: 40.2%, 40.5%, and 47.1%, only one of which is in New England. Since 1982, no large bank holding company whose share price fell below 40% of book value (and remained there for more than one calendar quarter) has survived more than eighteen months as an independent entity, without federal assistance, after reaching that level.
10. Hershey (1991) writes, "Treasury Under Secretary Robert R. Glauber took issue with Mr. Greenspan's assessment. Recapitalizing the [BIF] . . . is a liquidity issue, he said. 'Providing liquidity to the banking system is one of the primary traditional responsibilities of the Federal Reserve.' " In a sobering renewal of the Treasury's request for the $25 billion bailout loan from the Fed (May 29, 1991), Mr. Glauber told a House Ways and Means Subcommittee that he still saw no reason why the Fed should not make the loan. At this writing, Congress has not

incorporated this aspect of the Treasury request into pending legislation (Todd 1991).

11. About 75% to 80% of all commercial banks' U.S. deposits are insured, by dollar amount. However, at money center institutions, about one-half of all deposits are raised offshore and are technically uninsured, although the Federal Reserve, the FDIC, and the Treasury often decide to repay such deposits because of some combination of the "too big to fail" doctrine and concerns regarding the undefined term "systemic risk," which usually means direct interbank exposure. See Todd and Thomson 1990.
12. For a call to extend deposit insurance universally, coupled with expanded bank powers and closer supervision by the government, see *New York Times*, 1991.

References

Aristotle. *The Nichomachean Ethics*. Translated by J. E. C. Weldon. Buffalo, N.Y.: Prometheus Books, 1987.

Barnett, Randy E., ed. *The Rights Retained by the People*. Fairfax, Va.: George Mason University Press, 1989.

Benston, George J., et al. *Perspectives on Safe and Sound Banking*. Cambridge, Mass.: MIT Press, 1986.

Friedman, Milton, and Anna Jacobson Schwartz. *A Monetary History of the United States, 1867–1960*. Princeton: Princeton University Press for the National Bureau of Economic Research, 1963.

Greenspan, Alan. "Testimony before Senate Committee on Banking." *Federal Reserve Bulletin* 77, no.6 (June 1991): 430-43.

Hackley, Howard. *Lending Functions of the Federal Reserve Banks: A History*. Washington, D.C.: Board of Governors, 1973.

Hershey, Robert D., Jr. "Greenspan Is Cautious on Easing." *New York Times*, April 24, 1991, Cl. c5 (national edition).

Kane, Edward J. *The Gathering Crisis in Federal Deposit Insurance*. Cambridge, Mass.: MIT Press, 1985.

Knight, Jerry. "White House Plan to Bolster FDIC Dealt New Setback." *Washington Post*, April 24, 1991.

Mayer, Martin. "Too Big Not to Fail," *Forbes*, April 15, 1991, 68–71.

New York Times. "Driving Banks to Desperate Risks," April 14, 1991 (editorial).

O'Driscoll, Jr., Gerald P. "Deposit Insurance in Theory and Practice." *Cato Journal* 7 (Winter 1988): 661–75.

Todd, Walker F. "Lessons of the Past and Prospects for the Future in Lender of Last Resort Theory." Federal Reserve Bank of Cleveland, Working Paper No. 8805 (August 1988). Also in Federal Reserve Bank of Chicago,

Proceedings of a Conference on Bank Structure and Competition (1988).

———. "Why the Fed Should Not Bail Out the FDIC." Unpublished manuscript, 1991.

Todd, Walker F., and James B. Thomson. "An Insider's View of the Political Economy of the Too Big to Fail Doctrine." Federal Reserve Bank of Cleveland, Working Paper No. 9017 (December 1990).

Wheelock, David C., and Subal Kumbhakar. "Did Deposit Insurance Contribute to Bank Failures in the 1920s? Evidence from Kansas." Austin: Center for Economic Research, University for Texas Working Paper 91–02 (1990).

White, Eugene Nelson. *The Regulation and Reform of the American Banking System, 1900–1929*. Princeton: Princeton University Press, 1983.

White, Lawrence H. *Competition and Currency: Essays on Free Banking and Money*. New York: New York University Press, 1989.

6

The Diminishing Role of Commercial Banking in the U.S. Economy

George G. Kaufman

Commercial banking and depository institutions in general were one of the great financial innovations of all times. Indeed, it would be almost impossible to envision the modern complex economies of highly developed countries without a large and strong generic banking sector. But recent and rapid advances in technology and outmoded public policies have, on the one hand, reduced the historical comparative advantage of banks and, on the other hand, restricted the competitiveness and endangered the safety of banks. As a result, the importance of banking as an industry is being dramatically reduced. Although the longer-run implications of this erosion on the macroeconomy is neutral, as nonbank lenders provide additional credit, shorter-run implications may be less favorable to some sectors of the economy and are likely to lead to the adoption of some public policies that may trade short-term improvements for longer-term accelerated deterioration.

I. Introduction

Modern generic banking developed as economies passed through the commercial and industrial revolutions to encourage aggregate savings, improve the collection of savings, and make savings available to a wider range of potential borrowers. Before banking, savers (lenders) and borrowers had to search each other out and negotiate terms satisfactory to both parties. This process was time consuming, cumbersome, and inefficient. It frequently resulted in the failure to consummate agreements. In contrast, banks were able to tailor their securities more closely to the needs of almost every conceivable potential saver and borrower in terms of size, maturity, interest-rate sensitivity, default risk, currency of denomination, and prepayment or other options. They increased greatly the flow of funds from savers to borrowers.

In addition, both because banks provide a large number of other financial services to their loan customers and because they are specialists in lending, they were able to acquire more complete, timely, and private information about the credit quality of their customers and evaluate this information more accurately than most nonbank lenders. In other words, they were the major beneficiaries of asymmetrical information.

But the tailoring process led to a mismatch of the characteristics of the securities on the two sides of the banks' balance sheets. Of particular importance both to the management of the bank and to public policymakers was the mismatch in maturity and liquidity. For banks, the maturities of their deposit liabilities were shorter, on average, than those of their loan assets, and the liquidity was greater. Thus, the banks were vulnerable to solvency problems from unexpected adverse changes in interest rates and runs that led to sudden withdrawals of deposits. To protect against such problems, banks held sufficient capital and liquid reserves and managed their credit and interest rate exposures. Although throughout most of, at least, U.S. history, bank failure rates were not out of line with nonbank failure rates, the failures that did occur were highly visible and widely perceived to be more harmful to the community than the failure of a nonbanking firm of comparable size, particularly if the bank were liquidated.[1] Losses accrued to noteholders and depositors that, because bank notes and deposits accounted for the large share of the money supply, at times resulted in a decline in the money supply in the community, although not necessarily nationally if aggregate bank reserves were unaffected. The reduction in money in the community contributed to reduced spending in the community. In addition, loan relationships were interrupted, particularly in sectors such as business lending, in which banks had very large shares of the market. This also impacted the community adversely.

Bank runs and failures were also perceived to spill over to other banks as the complexities of bank balance sheets were believed to make it difficult for most depositors to differentiate financially healthy from financially sick banks. Because the costs of transferring or withdrawing deposits is small, depositors would prefer to be safe than sorry and run on other banks in sympathy. If the funds were not redeposited at other banks, either directly or indirectly, but held as currency outside the banking system, aggregate bank reserves declined and ignited a multiple contraction in money and bank credit. Thus, the difficulties at one bank, particularly a large bank, could infect other banks and adversely affect the economy at large.

The evidence suggests that these fears were more perceived than real and the costs greatly exaggerated. Nevertheless, through time as financial sectors became more important, banks became targets of progressively stronger prudential regulation, culminating in federal deposit insurance after the severe breakdown of the U.S. banking system in 1933. Unfortunately, the deposit insurance was structured perversely.[2] By reducing depositor discipline and not charging banks for greater risk taking, deposit insurance encouraged banks to run down their capital-asset ratios and increase the credit and interest rate risk exposures of their portfolios. Moreover, by guaranteeing the par value of deposits regardless of the solvency of the bank, the insurance discouraged depositors from running on insolvent banks and permitted insolvent banks to continue in operation until closed by the regulators. But regulators became increasingly reluctant to resolve insolvent banks, particularly larger banks, in a timely fashion, for numerous reasons. They feared potential spillover to other banks, loss of deposit and credit services to the community, and public embarrassment from admitting failure to protect safety. They faced political pressures from the banks' managers, shareholders, and even larger loan customers. Thus, in more recent years, the reduction in market discipline was not offset by an increase in regulatory discipline on problem banks.

In earlier years, when banks had a comparative advantage in their deposit and lending activities, there was widespread fear of excessive economic and even political power by banks. This fear was particularly strong in the United States and resulted in restrictions on their product and geographic powers. What better way to limit bank power than by limiting their growth by limiting their ability to enter additional product and geographic markets! Thus, unlike firms in other industries, banks were not permitted to operate branch offices, except where permitted by state law, and in no instances across state lines. This made it difficult for individual banks to follow customers who moved or to service customers with operations in distant places. When some banks attempted to circumvent these restrictions as recently as in the 1950s by crossing state lines through holding company affiliates, they were stopped in 1956 by the Douglas Amendment to the Bank Holding Company Act of that year.

Banks had always been restricted in the types of activities they could conduct within the bank or in subsidiaries of the bank by provisions of the bank charter granted by the federal government or the state. For example, national banks are restricted to

> all such incidental powers as shall be necessary to carry on the business of banking; by discounting and negotiating promissory notes, drafts, bills of exchange, and other evidences of debt; by receiving deposits; by buying and selling exchange, coin, and bullion; by loaning money on personal security; and by obtaining, issuing, and circulating notes according to the provisions of this chapter.

But they were not restricted in what affiliates of their parent holding companies could do until the enactment of the Bank Holding Company Act of 1956 and its extension to one-bank holding companies in 1970. In addition, the Glass-Steagall (Banking) Act of 1933 prohibited commercial banks from engaging in full-service investment banking. This act and the accompanying separation of "banking and commerce" were strongly supported by the Federal Reserve. It is of interest to note that the conventional-wisdom, "historical" separation of banking and commerce in the United States goes back only to 1956—indeed, only to 1970, which was the date of separation for all banks.

Similar to the restrictions on geographic locations, the restrictions on product activities prevented banks from participating fully in the provision of the many financial services that were innovated after the restrictions were imposed, in offering consumers a wide range of financial and nonfinancial services under one roof, and in being able to generate any synergies or economies of scope that would permit them to offer packages of services at lower cost. Their competitors, including foreign banks, generally were not similarly constrained.

The restrictions not only limited bank profitability but also increased bank risk by limiting the ability of banks to diversify either geographically or in product lines. Thus, the financial health of banks was closely tied to that of the local market area and the demand for the existing product lines. Before the 1920s for the geographic restrictions and the 1960s for the product restrictions, the adverse impacts of the regulations on the banking industry were not overly onerous, as the relatively primitive stage of technology did not favor wide geographic branch networks or wide product lines. Few banks took full advantage of the state branching powers that were available, the ability to acquire holding company affiliated banks in other states, or the ability to combine other financial and even nonfinancial activities within bank holding companies. But this experience changed dramatically in more recent years.

II. Erosion of Market Share

Commercial banks have been losing market share throughout most of the post-World War II period. In 1950, total assets of commercial banks represented more than one-half of the total assets of eleven major types of financial institutions (Table 6.1). By 1990, this market share had eroded to only 32%. Most of the decline occurred between 1950 and 1960 and may be attributed to a rundown of the unusual liquidity built up during World War II, when consumer spending was curtailed and interest rates were maintained at very low levels. Thus, the opportunity cost of holding noninterest yielding demand deposits was small, and nonbank institutions had few outlets for their funds.

But this unusual competitive advantage disappeared in the postwar economy. Since 1960, the erosion in the banks' market share has been slower, although it accelerated again in the 1980s. The rapidly gaining financial institutions were primarily private and public pension funds and money market funds. Life insurance companies have also experienced a major continuing erosion in market share. After first tripling their market share through the mid-1980s, savings and loan associations saw their share drop abruptly in 1989 and 1990 to the lowest percentage since the mid-1950s.[3]

The recorded loss in bank market share may be overstated, however, because the data do not include off-balance sheet activities, which tend to be greater for commercial banks than most other financial institutions. Moreover, market share is not necessarily equivalent to profitability, which is economically the more important. Some or all of any reduced income from reduced on-balance sheet activities may be offset by higher income from increased off-

Table 6.1
Asset Size, Relative Importance, and Market Share of Major Financial Institutions on the Intermediary Financial Market, From 1950–1990

	1990 Asset Bank	*Billions of Dollars*	*Percentage of Total Assets*				
			1950	*1960*	*1970*	*1980*	*1990*
Commercial Banks	1	3,358	52	38	38	37	32
Life Insurance Cos.	2	1,381	22	20	15	12	13
Private Pension Funds	3	1,140	2	6	9	12	11
Savings & Loan Assns.	4	1,106	6	12	14	15	11
State & Local Pension Funds	5	756	2	3	5	5	7
Finance Companies	7	580	1	3	4	2	6
Mutual Funds	6	641	3	5	5	5	6
Casualty Insurance Cos.	8	519	4	5	4	4	5
Money-Market Funds	9	499	-	-	-	2	5
Savings Banks	10	263	8	7	6	4	3
Credit Unions	11	213	-	1	1	2	2
Total		10,457	100	100	100	100	100

Source: Board of Governors of the Federal Reserve System, *Flow of Funds*, various years.

balance sheet activities.[4] Nevertheless, the apparent loss in the bank's market share may be attributed primarily to four factors: technological change, regulation, reversal of the federal deposit insurance subsidy, and quality deterioration.

Technological Change

As noted earlier, commercial banks historically have had an important comparative advantage over most other lenders. They had more complete and timely credit information about current and potential borrowers at lower cost. They obtained this information not only from the same sources as did other lenders but also from their own ongoing contacts with their customers through deposit, financial advising, safekeeping, and other relationships. This source was unique to the banks and greatly reduced the cost and increased the quality of their credit information for both the initial underwriting of a loan and the subsequent monitoring of its performance. As a result, many lenders found it more profitable to channel credit to borrowers through the commercial banking system indirectly than to buy the debt of the borrowers directly.

But this comparative advantage has been eroding in recent years due to technical advances in computers and telecommunications. Large and complete credit files on major borrowers are now readily available to almost everyone, quickly and at low cost. As a result, lenders are now finding it increasingly more profitable to buy securities directly from larger borrowers.[5] This accounts in part for the rapid increase in commercial paper issued by borrowers in recent years. In the ten years between year-end 1979 and year-end 1989, commercial paper issued by nonfinancial borrowers increased by more than 300%. In contrast, total bank assets increased only 140% and bank business loans only 100%.

Commercial banks and other depository institutions have traditionally also been able to collect funds from small and medium-sized lenders (savers) at low cost at branch offices at which they could also provide loan and other services to the same customers. This has permitted the banks to enjoy synergies that reduced the cost of gathering the deposits. However, the same recent advances in computer and telecommunications technology that made credit information more readily available to a wider population have also reduced the cost of collecting funds directly from small and medium-sized savers. Branch offices may be bypassed, and these offices have become increasingly more costly relative to funds collection via automatic, telephone, and wire transfers. As a result, many bank competitors can operate profitably on narrower margins. In response, banks have increasingly sold loans out of their portfolios and concentrated more on generating earnings from fees for loan originations than from loans held as portfolio investments. Technology has also made selling existing loans easier by making it possible to create the information and monitoring systems necessary to securitize packages of whole loans. Securitized loans are more marketable, more divisible, and more diversifiable than an equal dollar amount of whole loans and, thus, more desirable to nonbank investors.

Lastly, commercial banks have traditionally been granted a monopoly over demand (check-writing transfer) deposits by the government, and these deposits have been their major source of funds throughout most of banking history. But technology has now permitted almost anyone with access to large-scale computers and telecommunications to offer demand-deposit-like and rapid-funds transfer services. The monopoly has been undermined. Thus, money market funds, owned either independently or by nonbank financial and nonfinancial firms, have grown rapidly in recent years and have captured significant market share from the banks. Besides dampening their asset growth, this change has eroded the franchise value of banks and thus the market value of their capital.

Regulation

As discussed earlier, commercial banks are hampered in their ability to compete with their new nonbank competitors by excessive and outmoded government regulation of their product and geographic powers. Unlike most of their competitors, banks may not offer all types of financial services or most types of nonfinancial services. Thus, banks may not offer insurance underwriting, a full line of life and casualty insurance brokerage services at most offices, complete securities activities (except in recent years, relatively inefficiently, by the very largest banks through separate subsidiaries), retail merchandising, automobile manufacturing, and so on. Also, unlike their competitors, commercial banks may not operate full-service offices freely at any location of their choosing or in the organizational form that they may prefer. In many states, banks may operate branches only at limited locations and in no instances across state lines and have only recently been granted limited authority to operate full-service offices in other states in the form of holding-company affiliates. These restrictions have limited the profit potential both of individual banks and of the industry as a whole.

As noted, the reasons for these restrictions lie in the history of U.S. public policy toward commercial banks and in the primitive state of technology in earlier periods. But the recent advances in technology and increases in competitors that have reduced the market share of banks have also sharply reduced their potential for excessive concentration of power and abusive conflicts of interest.[6] As a result, the public policy concerns for restricting bank product and geographic powers appear to be less important today than in earlier years and justify a careful reexamination of the benefits and costs. Indeed, the major public policy concern being voiced currently against expanded product powers centers on the unfair and potentially costly use of insured deposits by banks to fund the new activities to the taxpayers. However, the efficient correction of this perceived problem lies in the appropriate reform of federal deposit insurance, rather than in restricting bank activities.

Restrictions of bank product and geographic powers have not

only contributed to reducing the banks' market share by limiting their expansion relative to that of their competitors but also by reducing the asset-to-capital multiplier that is consistent with safety. To the extent that product and geographic expansion results in increased diversification, bank risk is reduced and the market will permit banks to operate with greater leverage.

In addition, banks are prohibited from paying explicit interest on demand deposits and were restricted until ten years ago in the interest rate they could pay on smaller-time deposit accounts. The latter restriction, Regulation Q, was directly responsible for the establishment of money market funds, which have maintained a significant share of the market long after the regulation was removed.

Market forces do not necessarily wait for legislated liberalization of the restrictions, particularly at the federal level. Thus, effectively, all states have now adopted legislation to override the federal restrictions on interstate holding company imposed by the Douglas Amendment to the Bank Holding Company Act of 1956. Simultaneously, the regulatory agencies and the courts have combined to permit banks to offer an almost complete menu of securities activities.[7] But by limiting these activities to affiliates of the bank holding company and imposing restrictions on the relative volume of such activities to the bank's total securities activities, the current regulations effectively limit most of the newly granted activities to the country's largest banks.

Deposit Insurance

As has been amply documented in recent years, improperly structured federal deposit insurance substitutes public capital for private capital and permits banks to operate with greater private capital leverage than otherwise. To the extent that the evidence suggests that federal deposit insurance has been underpriced in recent years, it has permitted banks to maintain a larger asset base than otherwise for the amount of capital they had and aided banks in maintaining their market share. However, recent and proposed changes in the insurance structure are likely to reverse this situation. Capital ratio requirements are likely to be increased. Insurance premiums already have been increased substantially and may be increased even further. To the extent that the premiums are now higher than necessary for the insurance fund to be actuarially sound and are imposed to help finance past deficits in the fund, they may be viewed as a

Figure 6.1
Financial Insitution Capital Levels: Median Equity Capital-to-Total Asset Ratios (December 31, 1989)

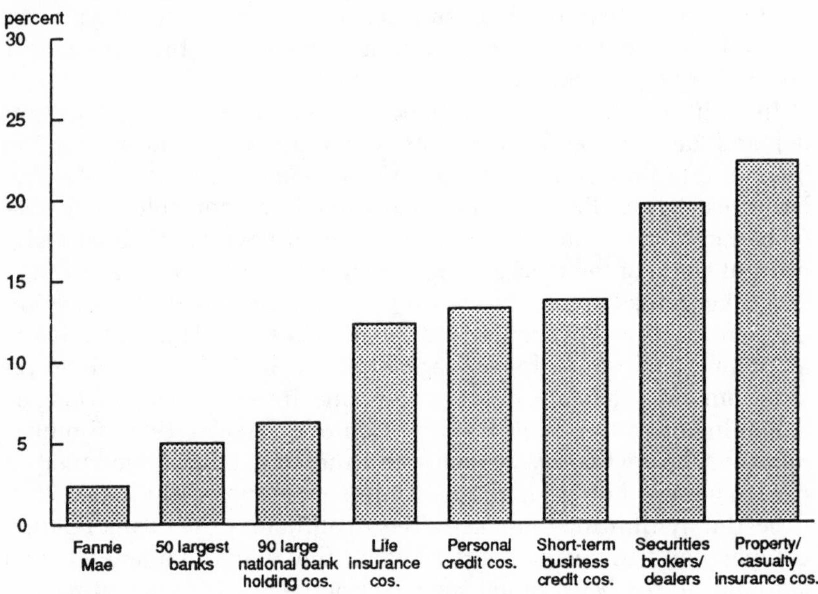

Source: U.S. Treasury Department, *Modernizing the Financial System* (Washington, D.C., 1991)

nonuser tax imposed on banks. Like any tax imposed on only some competitors and not on others, this tax increases relative costs and reduces the equilibrium output of the industry.[8]

At the same time that insurance premiums are being raised on banks, they are not being imposed on an increasingly significant competitor that is widely perceived to be also covered by the federal safety net. This competitor is the government sponsored enterprises (GSEs) that specialize in housing and agricultural finance, such as the Federal National Mortgage Association (FNMA), the Federal Home Loan Mortgage Corporation (FHLMC), and the Federal Agricultural Credit Association. Although they are privately owned and managed, these agencies have authority to borrow from the U.S. Treasury and their debt trades at interest yields higher than those of the U.S. Treasury but lower than those of comparable private firms.[9]

The lower interest rates indicate that the market perceives that there is a high probability that the federal government will not permit bondholders to suffer losses if the agencies encounter financial difficulties. This public perception is supported by the lower capital ratios of these firms relative even to commercial banks. As is shown in Figure 6.1, FNMA has a capital ratio of only 2.5%, less than one-half that of banks and less than one-fifth that of other financial industries. Moreover, if it were to evaluate FNMA as an independent entity without access to the Treasury, Standard and Poor's would have assigned it a rating of only A—in April 1991. Indeed, S&P would have assigned AAA ratings to only two of the five major GSEs (Federal Home Loan Banks and Sallie Mae) and a BB to one (Farm Credit System).[10]

Despite this perception, the government does not charge the agencies explicit or implicit (regulatory) insurance premiums. Thus, they have a cost advantage and are able to accept a lower return on their investments than are banks. To the extent that these investments compete with those made by banks, they reduce the profitability of banks and their asset size. Indeed, in the four years from 1987 through l990, FNMA, FHLMC, and Sallie Mae all averaged annual returns on equity in excess of 25%. This was three times the average 7.6% annual return for commercial banks and double the average 13% return for the S&P 500.[11]

It is sometimes argued that the deleveraging and consequent asset shrinkage associated with the higher private capital requirements being imposed on banks by regulators and legislators interferes with the continuation of healthy credit extension to businesses and households and produces a "credit crunch." To the extent that bank assets and therefore lending were greater than otherwise because of underpriced federal deposit insurance, a correction would reduce bank lending almost by definition. But this should not lead to a reduction in overall lending for economically sound projects by all institutions beyond a relatively brief transition period. Others, primarily the new bank competitors, should be able to expand their lending to offset any cutback by banks to borrowers who are willing and able to pay equilibrium market rates of interest, and new, adequately capitalized commercial banks would enter the arena if there were excess demand for unique bank credit at this interest rate.

This response would not differ greatly from the entry of, say, new grocery stores or the addition of grocery items to the services provided by previously nongrocery stores if individual grocery stores failed or were forced to cut back on storage space obtained temporarily from suppliers, but the demand for grocery products at a market price remained unchanged. Beyond the time necessary for the new providers to come on line, no "food crunch" would arise. In banking, the costs associated with the above transition, while significant for some borrowers and some sectors, are likely to be far less to the public as a whole than the costs of not correcting the existing combination of asset overcapacity and lack of market discipline that have contributed to the large increases in loan losses and bank failures.

Quality Deterioration

Historically, banks have had higher credit ratings and reputations than most borrowers. Thus, the addition of a bank's signature to a private borrower's note would enhance its credit quality. Borrowers with lower than the highest credit ratings could borrow at banks at no higher and even lower interest cost than borrowing directly from lenders. But the financial difficulties experienced by many commercial banks in recent years have changed this scenario. In part, the poor current financial condition of the banking industry reflects the inefficient deposit insurance structure in place, which has permitted banks to operate with very low capital ratios. In recent years, commercial bank capital ratios have been near 6% in book value and considerably lower in market value. In addition, particularly for larger banks, off-balance sheet activities are substantial, at times even larger in volume than recorded on-balance sheet activities. Yet, these are excluded from the published capital ratios. The low bank capital ratios relative to other financial industries is evident from Figure 6.1. It does not take much of an adverse shock to asset values to wipe out such small capital and drive a bank into insolvency. And the increased volatility in the macroeconomy during the past fifteen years stemming from the abrupt inflation-deflation cycle of 1978–1986 and the rolling regional and sectoral recessions has produced such shocks.

U.S. banks also appear to be in weaker financial condition than banks in other major countries. As is shown in Figure 6.2, in recent years the market has valued the capital of U.S. banks as a percent of assets lower than it has for British, German, Swiss, or Japanese banks. A recent study also reported that at year end 1990, all three of the largest Swiss banks had AAA ratings and only two of the eleven largest Japanese banks and none of the largest German banks had S&P or Moody's credit ratings of below AA. French and British

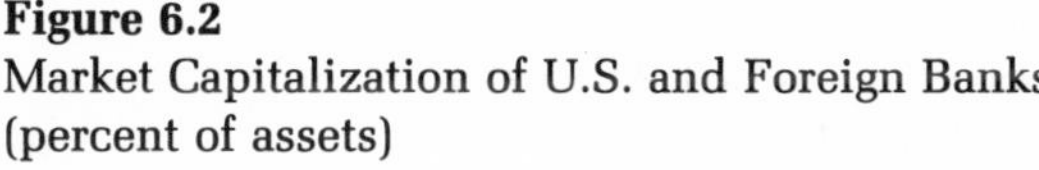

Figure 6.2
Market Capitalization of U.S. and Foreign Banks
(percent of assets)

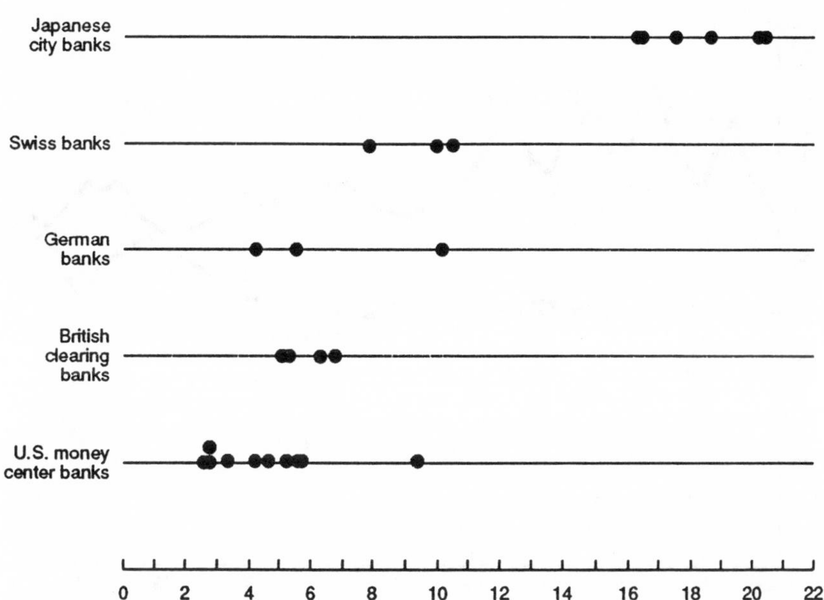

Source: Herbert L. Baer, "Foreign Competition in U.S. Banking Markets," *Economic Perspectives* (May/June 1990): 25.

banks were also rated highly. In contrast, only two of the eight largest U.S. banks had ratings of AA or above, and three were rated below A. Many other U.S. banks had even lower credit ratings.[12] The erosion of the credit quality of U.S. banks has been occurring throughout the 1980s. Ten years ago, S&P rated twelve large banks AAA. In 1991, only the Morgan Guaranty rated this rating. Over the same period, the average large bank credit rating deteriorated from a low AA to a low A-high BBB rating.

Because the credit quality of banks have been downgraded, an increasing number of large business borrowers now find it cheaper to borrow directly on financial markets, bypassing banks. It is not profitable for them to "intermediate down," and the demand for bank loan services is reduced. The downgraded credit quality of the banks, low capital ratios, and increase in failure rates may also have encouraged some bank loan customers to look to other types of institutions for a steady and dependable source of funds.

Figure 6.3
Real Estate and C&I Loans as a Percent of Total Loans
Insured Commercial Banks, 1939–1989

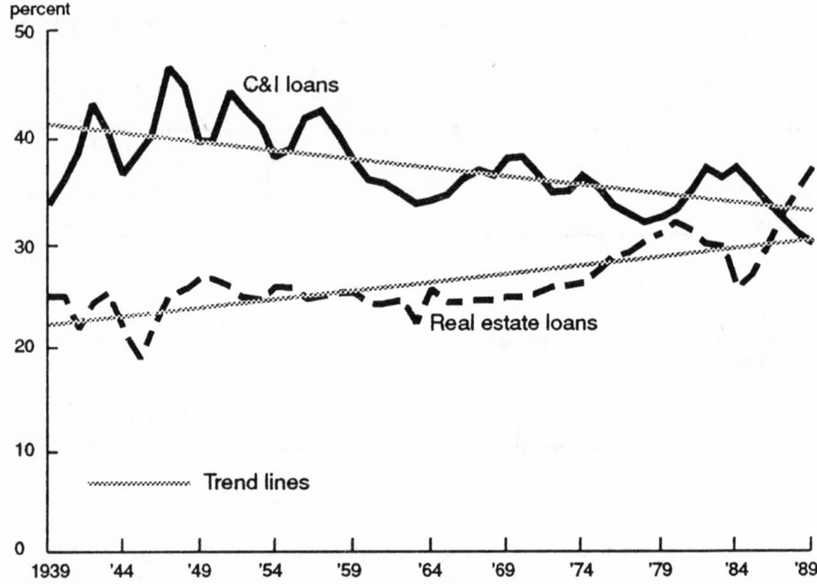

Source: U.S. Treasury Department, *Modernizing the Financial System* (Washington, D.C. 1991).

The result of such effects may be seen from the proportion of business loans made by banks, other financial institutions, and lenders directly in selected years from 1950 to 1989 shown in Table 6.2. The banks' share of loans to nonfinancial corporate business declined from near 90% in the immediate post-World War II period through the mid-1960s to near 80% in 1975, 70% in 1980, and only 60% in 1989. In contrast, funds raised through commercial paper increased from 1 to 12% in this period, loans from foreign sources from none to 8%, and loans from nonbank financial intermediaries from 6 to 16%. As a percent of bank business loans, commercial paper increased from only 10% in 1960 to nearly 100% in 1989. The longer-term decline in business lending by commercial banks is also evident from Figure 6.3. Since 1939, business loans have declined from 41% of total bank loans to 33% in 1989. In contrast, real estate loans have increased from 22% of total bank loans to 30%, or almost as important as business loans.

Table 6.2
Composition of Short-Term Credit Market Debt of Non-financial Corporate Business 1950–1989

	1950	*1960*	*1970*	*1980*	*1989*
			(Percent)		
Bank Loans	91	87	83	71	60
Nonbank Finance Loans	6	9	9	14	16
Commercial Paper	1	2	6	9	12
Foreign Loans	—	—	—	1	8
Bankers' Acceptances	2	2	2	5	4
Total	100	100	100	100	100
(Billion Dollars)	20	43	125	324	903

Source: Board of Governors of the Federal Reserve System, *Balance Sheet for the U.S. Economy, 1945–89*, October 1990.

III. Public Policy Implications

Why should the public be concerned with whether commercial banks, depository institutions, or any industry for that matter shrinks or even survives? Through history, many industries have diminished in size from their peaks and even disappeared altogether. Public policy should be concerned only if a contributing force to the decline is public policy itself or if, particularly in the short-run or transition period, the reduction in aggregate size has adverse effects on the economy as a whole or on important sectors. As was argued earlier, banking is rapidly losing its historical comparative advantage as a result of technological advances so that its eventual demise will not impact the macroeconomy greatly.

But its demise is being accelerated by public policies that both reverse the previous subsidy to growth from underpriced deposit insurance and place banks at an artificial competitive disadvantage relative to competitors, who in the absence of the constraints may not be more economically efficient suppliers. If this observation is correct, then extant public policy is encouraging a harmful misallocation of resources. Moreover, even though money and credit are fungible, there are transition costs if the curtailment of bank suppliers of credit is abrupt.[13]

Displaced creditworthy borrowers other than the very largest have to search for nonbank suppliers who are compatible both geographically and product-wise, and reestablish credit relationships. At the same time, potential nonbank suppliers have to gear up operationally both geographically and product-wise to inaugurate credit relationships. In the short term, some creditworthy borrowers are likely to be unsatisfied and a perceived "credit crunch" said to exist. The credit crunch may be reinforced within banking if increased prudential regulation in the form of, say, higher capital requirements are imposed and all banks are not able to attract additional capital on equal terms because of differences in their financial condition. Creditworthy borrowers at capital-deficient banks need to transfer their relationships to capital-sufficient banks, possibly some distance away and specializing in different credit types. All credit, even all bank credit, is not perfectly substitutable instantaneously.[14] Moreover, employees laid off by losing commercial banks are unlikely to find employment at gaining banks or other institutions immediately.

But public policies to increase aggregate or sectoral bank assets by reducing prudential regulations are likely to be counterproductive. They are likely to result in a temporarily larger but economically weaker banking sector that will increase its burden on the taxpayers so that the long-run costs will greatly exceed any short-run gains. Instead, public policy should be directed at removing the structural restrictions to the extent consistent with necessary prudential regulation and a competitive economy. The key is to reform federal deposit insurance both to price the insurance correctly and to restrict losses to the private sector.[15] This should lead to a lasting larger and stronger banking system consistent with both safety and preserving competition. If banking continues to lose market share in such an environment, then its erosion may appropriately be attributed to market forces only and its demise no loss to anyone but the industry itself and its few remaining customers. Can commercial banks survive in a brave new world of efficiently priced deposit insurance and broader product and geographic powers? It would be strange if the industry could not, even though all individual banks may not. The rapid growth of most nondepository financial firms indicates significant demand for their financial services. Moreover, this growth occurred without benefit of access to underpriced deposit insurance. As a result, as was shown in Figure 6.1, these industries operated with substantially higher capital-to-asset ratios than banks.

Moreover, banks in major countries also operate with substantially higher capital ratios, particularly when measured in market

Figure 6.4
Total Assets of Multinational Banking Organizations by Headquarter Country (1972 = 100)

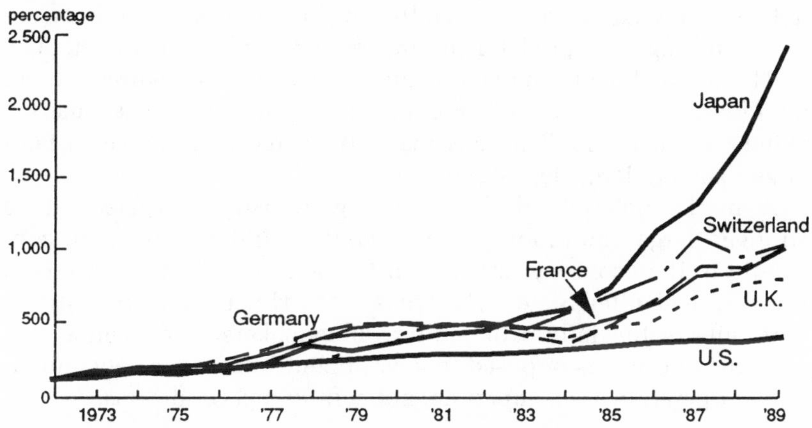

Source: George J. Benston, "U.S. Banking in an Increasingly Integrated and Competitive World Economy," *Journal of Financial Services Research* (December 1990): 315.

Figure 6.5
Total Assets of Multinational Banking Corporations Relative to GNP (1972 = 100)

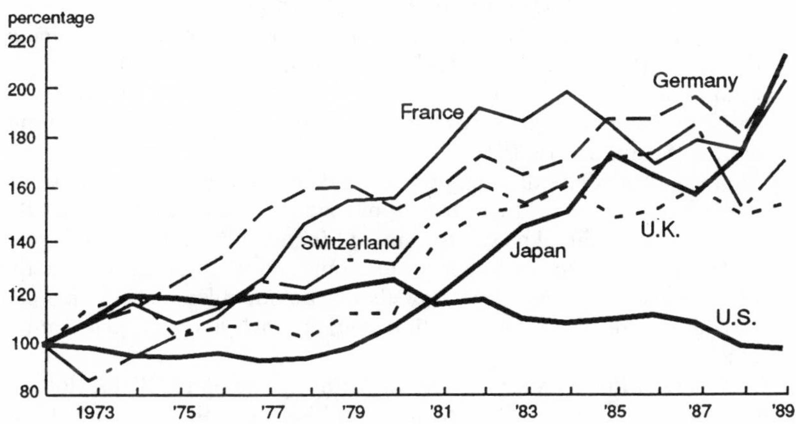

Source: George J. Benston, "U.S. Banking in an Increasingly Integrated and Competitive World Economy," *Journal of Financial Services Research* (December 1990): 316.

values. In most of these countries, banks have broader powers than in the United States. Indeed, the reason Japanese banks have been able to expand worldwide as rapidly as they have in recent years is not that they have used artificially low cost Japanese funds or engaged in long-term predator pricing, as is commonly claimed. (The asset growth of banks in major countries is shown in Figures 6.4 and 6.5.) Rather, as is evident in Figure 6.2, they had the highest market value capital ratios. This has made them more attractive to both large loan and large deposit customers.

A market-determined safer banking industry translates into a stronger, larger, and more efficient banking industry that can contribute to the economy rather than being a drag on it, as in recent years in the United States. The crisis in the U.S. banking industry in part reflects the failure of public policymakers to recognize that market-imposed, as opposed to government-imposed, safety and efficient operation are compatible, not conflicting, conditions.

Notes

1. George J. Benston, et al., *Perspectives on Safe and Sound Banking* (Cambridge, MA: MIT Press, 1986); and George G. Kaufman, "Banking Risk in Perspective," in George G. Kaufman, ed., *Research in Financial Services* (Greenwich, CT: JAI Press, 1989).
2. Edward J. Kane, *The Gatherinq Crisis in Federal Deposit Insurance* (Cambridge, MA: MIT Press, 1985); and Benston, et al.
3. George G. Kaufman, "The Incredible Shrinking S&L Industry," *Chicaqo Fed Letter* (Federal Reserve Bank of Chicago) (December 1990).
4. John H. Boyd and Stanley L. Graham, "Investigating the Banking Consolidation Trend," *Quarterly Review* (Federal Reserve Bank of Minneapolis) (Spring 1991): 3–15.
5. Some analysts deny that the private market can provide as much information as can banks. See Christopher James, "Some Evidence on the Uniqueness of Bank Loans," *Journal of Financial Economics* (December 1987): 216–35. On the other hand, some evidence suggests that the "uniqueness" of bank loans may also be obtained from other financial institutions on the intermediation market, such as insurance companies.
6. A review of these issues appears in Anthony Saunders, "Bank Holding Companies: Structure, Performance, and Reform," in William S. Haraf and Rose Marie Kushmeider, *Restructuring Banking and Financial Services in America* (Washington, D.C.: American Enterprise Institute, 1988), 156–203; Franklin R. Edwards, "Concentration in Banking: Prob-

lem or Solution?" in George G. Kaufman and Roger C. Kormendi, *Deregulatinq Financial Services* (Cambridge, MA: Ballinger, 1986), 145–68; and Richard J. Herring and Anthony M. Santomero, "The Corporate Structure of Financial Conglomerates," *Journal of Financial Services Research* (December 1990): 471–97.

7. George G. Kaufman and Larry R. Mote, "Glass-Steagall: Repeal by Regulatory and Judicial Reinterpretation," *Banking Law Journal* (September-October 1990): 388–421.
8. To the extent that there is excess capacity in banking, it is with respect to total assets in the industry, not to the number of banks. The latter is a function of any economies of scope, intensity of competition, and freedom of entry. Thus, mergers among banks will not automatically be profitable either for the participating banks or for societal welfare. A recent study found that few recent mergers among large banks proved successful over time for the shareholders of the participating banks relative to other banks. FMCG Capital Strategies, *Analyzing Success and Failure in Bankinq Consolidation,* Rolling Meadows, IL: Bank Administration Institute, 1990. See also Boyd and Graham.
9. For other lending activities covered by a federal safety net, see George G. Kaufman, "The Federal Safety Net: Not For Banks Only," *Economic Perspectives* (Federal Reserve Bank of Chicago) (November/ December 1987): 19–28; and U.S. General Accounting Office, *Government-Sponsored Enterprises: The Government's Exposure to Risk* (Washington, D.C., August 1990).
10. Secretary of the Treasury, *Report on Government Sponsored Enterprises* (Washington, D.C.: U.S. Treasury Department, April 1991), xxi.
11. Ibid., 1.
12. Randall J. Pozdena, "Recapitalizing the Banking System," *FRBSF Weekly Letter* (Federal Reserve Bank of San Francisco) (March 8, 1991): 3. See also George M. Salem, et al., *Banking Industry Outlook* (Prudential-Bache Securities) (December 31, 1990): 9–12.
13. The fungibility of credit is best evidenced by the conclusions of a recent study by the Federal Reserve Bank of Dallas that

> the upheaval suffered in the Texas banking sector had little effect on overall economic activity in the state. While we find evidence that economic events affected the banking sector, we can find little evidence that lending activity by Texas banks exerted any influence on overall economic activity. One possible explanation for these results is that capital apparently flows fairly well across regions. If Texas banks were either unable or unwilling to extend viable loans, then perhaps banks and other financial institutions outside the state fulfilled this function.

Jeffrey W. Gunther and Kenneth J. Robinson, "The Texas Credit Crunch," *Financial Industry Studies* (Federal Reserve Bank of Dallas) (June 1991): 6.

14. It is interesting to note that a credit crunch has not been perceived in residential mortgage lending despite the abrupt decline in the dollar assets and number of S&L associations. Kaufman, "The Incredible Shrinking S&L Industry."
15. George J. Benston and George G. Kaufman, *Risk and Solvency Regulation of Depository Institutions: Past Policies and Current Options* (New York: Salomon Brothers Center, New York University, 1988); George G. Kaufman, "A Proposal for Deposit Insurance Reform That Keeps the Put Option Out-of-the-Money and the Taxpayer in-the-Money," in Charles A. Stone and Anne Zissu, eds., *Risk Based Capital Regulations: Asset Management and Funding Strategies,* Business One Irwin, forthcoming; and Shadow Financial Regulatory Committee, "A Program for Deposit Insurance and Regulatory Reform," Statement No. 41, Chicago, Loyola University, February 13, 1989.

References

Benston, George J. "U.S. Banking in an Increasingly Integrated and Competitive World Economy." *Journal of Financial Services Research.* (December 1990): 311–86.

Benston George J., and George G. Kaufman. *Risk and Solvency Regulation of Depository Institutions: Past Policies and Current Options.* New York: Salomon Brothers Center, New York University, 1988.

Benston, George J., et al. *Perspectives on Safe and Sound Banking.* Cambridge, MA: MIT Press, 1986.

Boyd, John H., and Stanley L. Graham. "Investigating the Banking Consolidation Trend." *Ouarterly Review,* Federal Reserve Bank of Minneapolis (Spring 1991): 3–15.

Edwards, Franklin. "Concentration in Banking: Problem or Solution?" In G. G. Kaufman and R. C. Kormendi, eds., *Derequlatinq Financial Services.* Cambridge, MA: Ballinger, 1986. 145–68.

FMCG Capital Strategies. *Analyzinq Success and Failure in Bankinq Consolidation.* Rolling Meadows, IL: Bank Administration Institute, 1990.

Gunther, Jeffrey W., and Kenneth J. Robinson. "The Texas Credit Crunch," *Financial Industry Studies,* Federal Reserve Bank of Dallas (June 1991).

Herring, Richard J., and Anthony M. Santomero. "The Corporate Structure of Financial Conglomerates." *Journal of Financial Services Research* (December 1990): 471–97.

James, Christopher. "Some Evidence on the Uniqueness of Bank Loans." *Journal of Financial Economics.* (December 1987): 216–35.

Kane, Edward J. *The Gathering Crisis in Federal Deposit Insurance.* Cambridge, Mass.: MIT Press, 1985.

Kaufman, George G. "The Federal Safety Net: Not for Banks Only." *Eco-*

nomic Perspectives, Federal Reserve Bank of Chicago (November-December 1987): 19–28.

———. "Banking Risk in Historical Perspective." In G. G. Kaufman, ed., *Research in Financial Services*. Vol. 1. Greenwich, CT: JAI Press, 1989. 151–64.

———. "The Incredible Shrinking S&L Industry." *Chicago Fed Letter*, Federal Reserve Bank of Chicago. (December 1990).

———. "A Proposal for Deposit Insurance Reform That Keeps the Put Option Out-of-the-Money and the Taxpayers in-the-Money." In Charles A. Stone and Anne Zissu, eds., *Risk Based Capital Regulations: Asset Management and Funding Strategies*. Business One Irwin, forthcoming.

———. "Capital in Banking: Past, Present, and Future." *Journal of Financial Services Research* (April 1992): 385-402.

Kaufman, George G., and Larry R. Mote, "Glass-Steagall: Repeal by Regulatory and Judicial Reinterpretation." *Bankinq Law Journal* (September-October 1990): 388–421.

Pozdena, Randall J., "Recapitalizing the Banking System." *FRBSF Weekly Letter*, Federal Reserve Bank of San Francisco. (March 8, 1991).

Salem, George M., et al. *Banking Industry Outlook*. New York: Prudential-Bache Securities, December 31, 1990.

Saunders, Anthony. "Bank Holding Companies: Structure, Performance, and Reform." In W. S. Haraf and R. M. Kushmeider, eds., *Restructuring Banking and Financial Services in America*. Washington, D.C.: American Enterprise Institute, 1988. 156–203.

Secretary of the Treasury. *Report on Government Sponsored Enterprises*. Washington, D.C.: U.S. Treasury Department, April 1991.

Shadow Financial Regulatory Committee. "A Program for Deposit Insurance and Regulatory Reform." Statement No. 41, Chicago, Loyola University, February 13, 1989.

U.S. General Accounting Office. *Government-Sponsored Enterprises: The Government's Exposure to Risk*. GAO/GGD-9097. Washington, D.C., August 1990.

Contributors

Roger W. Garrision is Associate Professor of Economics at Auburn University. He has published more than a dozen articles on capital and business cycles, and the monograph *Austrian Macroeconomics: A Diagrammatic Exposition* (1978). He is currently working on his first book, tentatively entitled *The Macroeconomics of Capital Structure.*

Thomas Havrilesky is Professor of Economics at Duke University. He is well known as the coauthor and coeditor (with John T. Boorman) of several textbooks and collections of readings on money, banking, and macroeconomics. Much of his recent research, including the recent book, *The Pressures on Monetary Policy,* provides empirical evidence of the political influences on the Federal Reserve.

George G. Kaufman is the John F. Smith Professor of Finance and Economics at Loyola University of Chicago. He is the author of numerous journal articles and two current money-and-banking textbooks, and is a coauthor of *Perspectives on Safe and Sound Banking* (1986). He is an editor of the *Journal of Financial Services Research* and a member of the editorial boards of several other journals.

Gerald P. O'Driscoll, Jr., is Vice President and Economic Advisor at the Federal Reserve Bank of Dallas. He is the author of *Economics as a Coordination Problem* (1977) and many articles on monetary theory and the history of economics. He is the coauthor (with Mario J. Rizzo) of *The Economics of Time and Ignorance* (1985).

Richard M. Salsman is Vice President and Economist at H. C. Wainwright and Co., Economics, Inc., in Boston and an adjunct fellow of the American Institute for Economic Research. He is the author of *Breaking the Banks: Central Banking Problems and Free Banking Solutions* (1990). He lectures widely on money, banking, and economics.

Walker Todd is Assistant General Counsel and Research Officer at the Federal Reserve Bank of Cleveland. His work has appeared in the annual *Research in Financial Services* and elsewhere. His contribution to the present volume was written while he was on a leave of absence at the Gulliver Foundation in San Francisco.

Lawrence H. White is Associate Professor of Economics at the University of Georgia. He is the author of *Free Banking in Britain* (1984), *Competition and Currency: Essays on Free Banking and Money* (NYU Press, 1989), and numerous articles on the theory and history of unregulated money and banking. He is currently writing a book entitled *The Theory of Monetary Institutions*.

Index